HEARTFIRE

Ieva Wool

For more information: ieva.wool@gmail.com

First paperback edition January 2024

Book cover and design by Kozakura
Interior dragon by Beatrix Fleming

ISBN 978-1-7390696-0-5 (paperback)
ISBN 978-1-7390696-1-2 (ebook)

www.ievawool.com

HEARTFIRE

For Beatrix, Leo and Joseph

The early morning sun stretches cool fingers over the quiet willow glade. Its dispassionate rays shimmer on sparkling dew, pale spring buds, torn wings, crumpled bodies, and pools of blood. Marielle, the Fae Queen-to-be, slumps awkwardly in the arms of her Captain. She is covered in blood from the devastation wreaked by a crossbow bolt piercing her chest.

Gravely wounded himself, the Captain of the Guard spends the last of his strength in a futile attempt to portal back to Hummingbird Clan village, where healers might save her.

As she releases her last, faint breath, no one hears the receding hoofbeats nor the shout, "Idiot! you weren't supposed to kill her, there's no ransom in that!"

From the village nestled in the trees not far away, a howl of despair rises up over the forest, as the Hummingbird Clan awakens to their unimaginable loss.

The Guards' horses stamp uneasily at the edge of the clearing.

CHAPTER 1

Yes!

I leap, twirl, *flicker*. I vanish between the dapples of sunlight in my birch grove and touch down on the other side. Again. Leap, twirl, *flicker*. Three times. Four.

I leap. I disappear. I land several paces away. I'm the youngest dancer ever to master *flicker*. It's breathtaking. I should be thrilled. Except it's all for nothing. I groan and stagger on the last landing, grabbing the nearest tree trunk to keep my balance.

I look down to check my wings, curving skirt-like around me, careful not to tear them on the peeling bark. They'll be really mad if I hurt my wings the day before I leave my Hummingbird Clan village for Queensdale. They'll be mad, anyway. I'm supposed to be back in our treetop village, studying. Learning governance and diplomacy instead of perfecting dance moves here in the forest.

Marielle, my cousin, my best friend. She loved all that stuff. My heartfire is just as strong as hers, but she was the one who was good at history. She used to tease me about having fluff inside my head as well as outside. I choke back a sob. She's gone.

She was meant to be Queen of the Fae, and I was meant to be a dancer. But now I'll never….

I catch a glimpse of orange, as a wizened old woman bursts into my glade, her hand raised, baring a scrawny stick of arm poking out from her sleeve. A ragged orange blanket is clasped at her shoulder and bundled on her back. A mottled wine-colored scarf tying back her hair writhes even though there's no breeze in the forest. She bustles toward me, leaning on a plain wooden staff in her other hand. The staff is not menacing, but the angry scowl on her face is.

Dammit! What's she doing here? Has she been watching me? I hastily retract my wings into their nubs on my shoulder blades and press myself into the crevasse between two birch trunks. I try to compress, to shutter the glow I always exude when I dance.

But the old woman steps closer, arm still raised. She points her long nose up at me and squints. "Good, it's you," she barks, "What are you doing so far from the village?"

My eyes flatten in exasperation. She must be the Human servant of one of the senior Clan Healers. My glow is gone, along with my wings as I imagine how mad the teachers will be when they find out where I've been—sneaking out to my secret glade, pretending for one last time that I'm a dancer, and trying to forget I'll never live up to the regal and intelligent Marielle.

"They're looking all over for you. Raiders have been spotted in the valley."

Fear and guilt clutch my stomach. Fear of the Raiders and what they would do to one like me, and guilt that Clan elders have to waste time searching for me when they should be preparing defenses.

"Come," she says, reaching her hand towards me. She's almost as tall as I am, tall for a Human, and I hop down from the tree to take a step toward her, hand meeting hand.

Too late, I remember safety rule number one: Never touch a stranger. Suddenly she yanks me off my feet with unbelievable strength, and tosses me over her shoulder into the mangy orange blanket that's really a sack.

I kick and scream and try to get out, but I can't find the opening. The sack is huge. Or maybe I'm shrinking. Or the old woman is much bigger than she appeared. My voice is shrinking too, it sounds far way. I'm terrified, mad, dizzy, and suddenly overcome by drowsiness. Some part of my brain realizes there must be sleeping powder in here. I feel the bumping of her walk, but then it fades, smooths, and I black out.

I struggle up out of an angry dream. Someone's shouting at me. *"It's your duty. For all the Clans."*

My brain is like porridge, my eyes feel hot. I open them a crack. I'm woozy—am I sick? Was it a party last night? Did I drink too much brambleberry wine?

I smell cabbage. Someone is humming tunelessly in a croaky voice. I open my eyes the rest of the way. There's nothing I recognize. I'm lying close to the floor. I can see a heavy table leg near my face, and a big wooden chair with arms. A figure in a burlap skirt shuffles to a fireplace. There's a battered round pot hanging on a chain over the fire. A scrawny arm stirs the pot with a big wooden spoon. The arm is attached to an old woman. That's who's humming.

I groan. The burlap skirt shuffles closer, goes away, comes back. A bony hand puts a bowl and a small wooden spoon on the floor beside me. "Here," the croaky voice says, "eat."

I lean up on one elbow. It's cabbage soup. It tastes strange, but I'm hungry and I gobble it down. The bowl and spoon slip out of my hand onto the floor, and I'm out.

I wake up. It's hot. My mouth is dry, my skin feels clammy and itchy, and my muscles are stiff. I'm lying on a straw-filled pallet on the floor. The old woman shuffles over and peers down at me. "Get up. Sit there," pointing to a stool. She takes a ladle of what's in the pot and serves it up in a bowl. Gives me a wooden spoon. The cabbage is hot, and strangely spiced. I eat. I sleep.

I wake again. I feel shaky. There's something I need to do, something I need to know.... I look around, dazed, muddled.

"Where am I? Who are you? How long have I been sleeping?"

"Six days and five nights," she says. "I carried you for two days. You're heavy."

There's something else I need to ask, but I can't remember what it is.

She keeps me indoors for days, maybe weeks—I don't know—except when I need to use the outhouse.

The cottage is as drab as the old woman. Its one room has a stone fireplace holding the round pot. Its walls slope downward from a peak. A window beside the door reveals the forest outside and lets in light during the day. The opposite wall holds a large rack bearing bundles of dried herbs, and there is a ragged orange burlap rug hanging behind it. A rough-hewn table sits near the center, holding bowls, clay pots and plants—grasses, flowers, roots, herbal medicines and some I don't recognize. I know a lot of them, but I don't know why.

There's something else I don't know. I don't know who I am.

I spend many hours near the lowest edge of the sloped roof, usually dozing or asleep on the itchy straw pallet. Most of my dreams are filled with yelling and crying, but sometimes I dream of dancers, their beautiful gossamer wings twirling as they *flicker* in and out of sight. I wake up reaching out my hand, my body yearning to move with them, but they evaporate and I'm left alone with the old woman.

Her sleeping pallet sits at the opposite side of the cottage. When she's not shuffling around the room, she sits on the big wooden chair near the table, her feet propped up on a three-legged stool. I'm not allowed near the big table. I eat at a small table with a broken leg crudely splinted with a birch branch.

By now I've figured out she puts sleeping powder into my soup, or porridge. Maybe I shouldn't eat it, but I'm hungry and there's nothing else. I dully wonder if I'm being held captive, if anyone is looking for me. Somewhere inside a voice is keening, terrified, but mostly I'm numb, and dozy.

She usually ignores me, humming about the room or working with the herbs at the table, muttering. A couple of times, I've seen her looking at me with a worried look, but she turns away when she notices me watching her.

"What's your name?" I ask another time when I have enough wit to think about it. She ignores me, or doesn't hear. I try again, louder. "What's your name?"

She glances at me sharply and points her finger. "Shush." I'm silenced, incurious, and doze off again.

Days pass by in a dingy haze. But sometimes I notice things. On the way back from the outhouse, the cottage looks like a tumble-down hut, obscured in shadow even though it's a sunny day. It's a bit hard to make out, and my gaze slides off it as nothing worth noting. It seems very small compared to the room inside. Staring at it gives me a queasy feeling in my stomach. I'm not sure how I know this, but I recognize that it's been placed under an illusion, a glamour.

One day, while she's out, I see that the orange rug hanging on the wall behind the rack of herbs is moving slightly, as though disturbed by a breeze. Even though I'm sluggish, I'm curious enough to examine it closer. I hold my hand near the edge of the rough burlap. Definitely air movement. I slide my hand behind it. Solid wall. Same thing on the other side. I try to slide the rack over to one side. It's very heavy, or maybe I'm just weak. I've managed to shift it a couple of inches when her barking laugh makes me jump and shriek.

"So, you've found my cupboard." She strides over, grabs the rack and tosses it to the side as if it weighed nothing. She lifts the rug. Nothing but wall. She looks at me and grimaces, and I realize she's trying to smile. She picks up the rack again and slides it to the other side. This time when she pulls back the rug, there's a large cupboard door. I reach toward a hole near the edge to pull it open.

"Go ahead," her grimace turns into a wide, lopsided grin. Inside is almost as wide as the outhouse, and about the height of my waist. "You should know about this, if you ever need to hide." She grabs me and shoves me into the cupboard. "Shush when you're in here. No calling, no knocking, no crying, no sneezing. You'll be safe. Remember this. You might need it one day."

I look up at her before I get out. The questions pile up, suddenly feeling urgent. Who is she? Why am I here? Who am I? And something else nagging at the back of my brain—what is it?

The days blur by, but I'm not sleeping all the time anymore. My body feels stiff from so much inactivity, so I start stretching my arms and legs and back to limber up. It feels like a practiced routine, but for what? My confusion mingles with a dull fear and growing anger toward this old hag who's keeping me here, but why?

At some point, she gets me to stir the pot and build up the fire when needed. She shows me how to tie up the bundles of herbs. It doesn't seem correct, but I can't think of another way to tie them.

Once in a while, I catch a few glimpses of memory. A village in the trees, dancers, long draping wings. Always that nagging feeling that there's something I'm supposed to be doing. But mostly it's sleep, and porridge, and cabbage soup.

I give up trying to ask her name. Not knowing just adds to my confusion. And growing anger. So, I start calling her Ragana. She doesn't seem to mind. My own name, I dunno. I guess I have one. Suh... Suh... Silly? But mostly I'm muddled, drowsy, passive.

The days become balmy. There's more to eat from her garden. Ragana sends me out to gather cabbage, corn, beans, radishes, carrots, peas. I stop to stretch my leg, pointing my toes out to the side. Then the other side. It feels good. Familiar. I nibble on a few berries from the edge of the garden, savoring their tartness. A beehive on the other side gives off a quiet buzz. I bathe in its soft chorus, and the warmth of the sun comforts me. I place my hands on the ground, as though I could *feel* into the earth.

I collect honey to sweeten our daily porridge, which she also uses for some flat cakes that she bakes at the edge of the fireplace. She stores them in a carrysack beside the door. I'd like a taste, but she doesn't give me any, and I don't ask.

One morning, a loud banging startles me awake and shakes the whole cottage. Ragana scurries me into the cupboard faster than I've ever seen her move. She grabs my sleeping pallet, shoves it in with me, and slaps the door shut. I hear her shuffle to the door, and the stomping of several pairs of feet.

CHAPTER 2

"What do you want?" Her voice is muffled by the cupboard and the rug over the door.

"Fairy," a gruff voice, unfamiliar accent "She wants Fairy. Give."

She? Who is She? Who are they? Are they trying to kidnap me? Rescue me? Stomach clenched, I hold my breath so I can hear better, but the pounding of my heart almost drowns out all other sounds.

"She's not here. She got away."

"You catch. They see you carry sack."

"I caught a lamb, fool. I cooked it in my stew pot."

My ears straining, I'm trying not to suffocate in the cupboard that's getting hotter and hotter. *Lamb stew. Omygods I've been eating meat.* I choke on the vomit that rises to my throat, trying not to spew all over myself. I feel so sick that I don't hear any more of what's said. Then there's banging and scuffling. And shouting.

I'm working so hard not to throw up, I don't notice when it gets quiet. Eventually, my stomach stops trying to hurl and my breathing slows down. I pat the blanket, reassured that it's dry. It's really stuffy, but I'm ok. It's too quiet. I wait for her to come and get me. She doesn't. I press my ear to the door. Nothing but a faint rasping sound, like someone slowly sanding wood. I doze off.

I come awake slowly. My legs feel cramped, and I realize I'm stuffed in the cupboard with my knees up to my chin. It takes me a minute to remember why I'm here. My head is more clear but the stale air discourages me from taking a deep breath. And I have to pee.

It's dark in the cupboard. No slivers of light from the cracks in the door. It's quiet. Ragana still hasn't come to let me out. I wonder how long I'll have to wait. The faint rasping sound is still there. I sleep again.

Next time I wake up with a start. I feel scared, claustrophobic. My heart is hammering in my chest. She said I'd be safe in here, and I haven't made any noise. Have the ruffians gone? Has she gone? I'm hungry. Afraid to move. Brain more clear but churning. I stick my finger through the little hole in the door. My fingertip touches the rug over the door. I give it a poke. Wait. Nothing. I poke it harder. Still nothing.

Swallowing panic, trying not to hyperventilate, I wiggle myself and the sleeping pallet around, drawing it under me so I'm not so squished. I kneel on it and put my eye against the hole. Complete darkness. I can't just sit here forever, so I call softly "Hello?" Nothing. Louder, "Are you there?"

Listening hard, I can hardly hear over my pounding heart. Is that a groan? I call again. Definitely a groan. I put my mouth to the hole, "Help...." Suddenly I'm panicking, desperate to get out. I push and pound on the door, which doesn't budge. I push as hard as I can, but it's not going to move. I'm trapped in here by the rug, and the rack of dried herbs leaning against the wall. I call out, "Ragana, is that you? How do I get out?"

Ear to the hole, I hear another muffled sound. Something like "Ash...."

"What? Say it again, please." I hold my breath.

I hear her voice faintly, "Lash. Be kind."

Dammit, what's she saying? Another try, her voice getting weaker. But on the third try, I decipher it. "Latch, behind."

I wriggle around again, so I can face the back of the cupboard. I feel around with both hands, but there's only the door, and the floor of the cupboard. I try to stifle my growing panic, getting desperate, when my fingers finally find a small loop of twine attached to a stick poking out of a corner near the floor. Panting, I pull and push, bending it up and down and to the sides, almost ready to give up when I give it a push and twist and I hear a click.

Suddenly there's air. Cool air. The back of the cupboard is also a door. I give it a shove and a crack opens. I breathe. I can smell the forest behind the cottage, and a faint whiff of outhouse. I listen and wait.

Nothing. I slowly push the door open and squeeze out. Pale moonlight shows my way, and I pause to listen every few steps. Only the night sounds of small animals and owls. I hurriedly visit the outhouse, then manage to inch around to the front of the cottage without tripping. The door is hanging open from one hinge.

Inside it's dark, the rasping noise is louder. There's no fire in the hearth, and a metallic smell in the air. I creep along the edge of the wall to find a candle and flint by the fireplace. I clumsily light it and...

Oh gods, there's blood, lots of blood. Ragana is lying on the floor, one leg at a weird angle. Her head is all bloody and one eye swollen shut.

CHAPTER 3

Caden lounges back in his chair at the well-worn tavern table, enjoying the good ale and the camaraderie of his friend Vincent. The window between them looks out over the town square of First Bend, where a horse patiently waits as its driver unloads a wagon of goods for the trading post. It also shows the town hall, where the Elders' Council decides on matters of governance. A milliner's shop sits on the other side, and beyond that a tiny shrine to the ancient gods, forgotten by most, though it still has a few devoted adherents. Further down, toward the edge of town, is the Ranger's compound where Caden has recently completed his training to help keep the town and surrounding forest free from danger.

First Bend sits nestled in the curve of a river that courses down from Raven's Peak Mountain, then flows on to Raven's Harbor, where it opens out to the sea. Upriver, three mountains, Raven's Peak, Dragon's End, and Cougar Mountain, encircle the large valley of Queensdale.

Vincent is a trader, on one of his regular visits to town. They have known each other since Caden was a child, and he always brings interesting and amusing anecdotes about the bustling seaport of Raven's Harbor and its merchants.

Vincent grows more serious as he moves on to a new subject. "A Fae has gone missing, a young female."

Caden sits forward, leaning his well-muscled arms on the table, and his gaze intensifies. He has the narrow face, wide brow, and violet eyes of a Fae, though his amber complexion and the slight upward curve of his eyes reveal a mixed heritage. His dark hair is caught back and hangs down over his leather jerkin.

He puts down his ale and listens closely. "This is intriguing news. I've never heard of the Fae asking Humans for help."

Although rulers of the Land, the Fae mostly keep to themselves, usually ignoring the affairs of their Human neighbors, unless there's a specific cause. But he's also heard they have few offspring, so they must be desperate.

But two seasons? She's been missing since early spring, and the leaves are already turning. She could be anywhere. Caden's seeking instinct is roused. He continues to listen to the trader, but one part of his mind is already questing as it does when he's sensing in the forest for game, or patrolling for Raiders.

A fleeting memory latches onto his mind. A grizzled old hermit who comes to town to get drunk once or twice a year. He's bedraggled and not very coherent, stooped over his ale. He's muttering about an old hag and how she must be hiding something.

Then his memory shifts to an occasionally seen hut half way up Cougar Mountain, the nearest of the three peaks he's patrolled as a Ranger. The hut, he recalls, seemed to deflect curiosity. Nothing seemed amiss, so he minded his own business, but the place had an air of cultivation even as his eye would slide off it. And he sensed, rather than saw, a haggard presence and a glimpse of orange burlap among the trees.

"What's her name, this Fae child?" he asks, interrupting the story.

"Sislie."

"How old?"

"Not a child, she's fully fledged."

So, her wings have grown. Definitely not a child. "Which Clan?"

"Hummingbird."

Caden nods, thinking. Hummingbird Clan is one of the High Clans that rule the Land, part of some complicated lineage that he's never paid attention to. They're known to be tall in stature, renowned diplomats, healers and also dancers. Last spring, they suffered the tragic loss of their Queen-to-be, Marielle, murdered on her way to Queensdale. So this second loss must be devastating.

His father may be from that Clan. The unknown father who gave him the intense violet gaze, narrow jaw, generous mouth and longish nose, which does not detract from a certain raffish good looks that he is oblivious to, but tends to induce shining eyes and rosy cheeks in the young women of the village—though their parents discourage them from romancing with the half-Fae, who are thought to be unreliable husbands.

Also from his father is the ability to sense what isn't shown. He sits very still, fully listening. "Tell me the rest."

"She appears to be rebellious and willful. Her parents say there's a birch grove where she'd practice enchantments and glamours, or illusions, and a special dance move unique to her

Clan. I've never seen it, but apparently, they can *flicker* out of sight as they leap and twirl."

Caden's eyebrows rise. He has seen this spectacular maneuver once, when his fellow Rangers brought him to a Moon Festival at Queensdale. They weren't invited into the palace, but during the outdoor festivities, one of the dance troupes included *flicker* in their performance. The dancers would leap and twirl, disappearing from sight, then instantly land a distance from where they started, still twirling. It was breathtaking.

Vincent continues, "She's a gifted dancer, as well as a healer. Also, she has some special status which they wouldn't talk about. She's fair of skin, curly blonde hair with a trace of red. Violet eyes."

Eyes the same color as his, though he has dark hair and beard from his mother's heritage. Now his wide brows are furrowed in concentration. "What else?"

"The hummingbird tattoo. Not really a tattoo, but a kind of sigil, or emblem. I understand the Fae all have one on their shoulder."

This is new. A sigil. He'll ask his mother if she knows anything about that.

"Sislie." As he says the name, something chimes in the center of his head. He startles and looks around to see where the sound is coming from. But Vincent shows no sign of having heard. He has more to say about what she was wearing, and other details that Caden makes note of without further comment.

Caden thanks his friend for the story, finishes his last sip of ale, and stands up. "I'm of a mind to go look for this Sislie."

Vincent clears his throat and says quietly, "There's one more thing. They are offering a handsome reward." He looks at his friend. "We've known each other for a long time and wouldn't usually ask for compensation. But I learned about this in the course of doing trade, so it's only fair that I ask for a share of the reward, if you find the young female." At Caden's lifted eyebrow, he continues, "how about a tenth of the reward?"

"That sounds fair. It's not just an idle tale you bring." They grasp each other's forearm in the Human custom, and Vincent returns to the market square to ply his trade.

Caden stays behind at the tavern to ask about the drunken hermit. The tavern keeper remembers him but knows nothing more, nor do any of the other townsfolk. Nor does the old whore, who is mostly interested in nattering on about an accident she had, involving a goat and a pail.

CHAPTER 4

Striding up the gently rising, forested path out of the village, Caden muses about Sislie. How could she just disappear? And what was that feeling/sound when he said her name? It feels like a geas, a compulsion, to go and find her. Where did that come from? Vincent said she's fully fledged, so her wings are developed, those strange wings the Fae don't use for flying, but are said to have powers. Though he's rarely seen them, since they almost always keep them retracted.

Lost in thought, and uncharacteristically oblivious to his surroundings, Caden barely acknowledges his neighbor Jacob's greeting. But as he draws near the toward the peaceful country home he shares with his mother, he comes back to himself.

The house sits back from the road. It has a wide sloped roof, and a generous veranda where he likes to enjoy an ale on summer evenings. Its chimney is built of river stones, as is the low fence that separates their land from the road. Arriving home, Caden always appreciates the wanton beauty of his mother's garden, populated by bees, butterflies and birds, where flowers and vegetables mingle happily and abundantly. She's at the back tending one of the beehives, crooning softly to soothe any alarm they might have at the Human intrusion. She glances his way and waggles her fingers to say she'll just be a minute.

He steps up onto the veranda, and into the house that has always been their haven. Its furnishings are simple but comfortable, the main room lined with shelves of many-colored fabrics and yarn. His mother's harp beside the fireplace lends extra grace. He has spent many companionable hours making music with her as he was growing up, joining her harp with his wooden flute as they played jigs and folk tunes, adding simple or complex harmonies as the mood would take them.

He pours himself a mug of the floral tisane she always keeps warm on the stove, and sits down at the wide table beneath the window that looks out over the veranda and the front of the house.

Moriko comes in from the garden, and hugs her son. She releases her long black hair from its kerchief and loosely braids it to hang over her shoulder, fastening it with a wooden clasp. She pours herself some tisane, takes a clump of wool to tease from a large basket, and joins him at the table where he sits leaning on his elbows.

Like her son, she has clear amber skin, a shade darker than most of the people in and around First Bend. Her eyes are deep brown and curve slightly upward. Features from the grandfather she never knew. And one of the reasons the townsfolk tend to keep their distance. That, plus her half-Fae son of an unknown father. But they happily buy the honey Moriko brings to market, and the wealthier farmers and merchants eagerly commission capes, blankets and other weavings she makes for their families. Once, a pair of handmaids of Maelys, Queen of the Fae, brought her a special turquoise dye and commissioned a delicate fabric for her mid-winter Moon Festival gown.

"Where are you off to this time?" She can always tell when her son is caught up in an adventure. Even though he has only recently qualified to be a full Ranger, she trusts him to stay safe. Her idea of safe is often different from his, but even so.

He sits back in his chair. "Vincent told me about a missing young female of the Fae. She may have been kidnapped. I'm going to go look for her."

She looks thoughtful. "This is a rare occurrence. There was a troubling rumor long ago, before you were born. A Fae disappeared, a small child. But the Fae keep their business to themselves."

"This is not a child. She's fully fledged, and has an adventurous personality." He leans forward, eyes bright in anticipation. "There's a reward too. If I find her, we could buy you that new loom you've been wanting, and some better dye vats for your wool. And I could build you a bigger shed to overwinter the sheep."

She sets her wool aside and takes his hands in hers. "I'm lucky to have a son like you, looking out for me, and not just chasing adventures."

Caden loves his mother and their home, but he lives for scouting the mountains and valleys near their village, with the freedom to roam, hunt and explore. But being a Ranger has responsibilities. More than once, he has warned wolves and cougars away from flocks of sheep that stray too close to the edge of the forest. He and the other Rangers light beacon fires in the mountains if they spot evidence of Raiders, the descendants of pirates that were shipwrecked on the rocky shores beyond the three mountains that encircle Queensdale valley. These Raiders, or Rocky Shorelanders, as they call themselves, inhabit the other side of the peninsula. They think nothing of stealing from townsfolk, or forcibly wooing young women who are rarely heard of again.

And he occasionally sees the elusive Fae. They are disdainful of Humans and have scant need for commerce. He has had little contact with them, even though he's half Fae himself. Many of them live in elaborately constructed tree villages in the densest part of the forest, with intricate systems of ladders and rope bridges. Other Clans live nestled in deep mountain canyons. The villages are usually obscured from Human sight with a glamour, or illusion, of Unnoticeability, which causes the eye to slide off and makes them blend into their surroundings unless someone stumbles upon them by accident. Except Caden. He and the few others with Fae blood can tell where they live. But he respects their privacy. In any case he wouldn't be welcome, since they'd consider him a clumsy half-breed.

"She's from the Hummingbird Clan, name of Sislie."

Moriko looks at him sharply, putting down the clump of wool she's started combing to ready it for the spindle. "Might be better to stay away from those ones."

"Ya Ma, I know he's probably one of them. You don't have to worry that I'll try to contact my father." His back stiffens, and he turns away from her so she won't see his angry scowl, their usual companionable space disrupted by the sulky feeling that takes him back to when he was the kid with few friends, that village youths used to bedevil without mercy. "I don't want to know that useless shirker, anyway."

"They don't like outsiders nosing in their business."

"I'm not nosing. They offered the reward."

"Alright then. But be careful." She presses her lips together and sets her wool down in a basket on the floor. "Bring that new jacket I made for you, it's getting colder."

"My old one's perfectly fine..." he pauses at her glance, remembering the sight of wrists sticking out of his sleeves. "Oh, ok, I grew again. Um, she apparently has a mark on her shoulder, a sigil. A hummingbird."

She looks out the window with a faraway gaze and speaks softly, "The Clans each have their own sigil—hummingbird, falcon, squirrel, lynx. It has to do with their unique powers, but I don't know much else. The hummingbird will be slightly iridescent." Her eyes down as she holds out her hand, "about the size of her palm."

Fascination and gratitude balloon in his chest. Their close relationship hasn't usually involved keeping secrets from each other, except for this. It's the first time she's ever volunteered information about the Fae, his father, or his Clan. She tells more, how the Hummingbird Clan are diplomats, healers, intelligent, also fine musicians and dancers.

"If you look closely at the sigil, there may be a small flame in the hummingbird's heart. This would mean she's a healer." Restless, she gets up from her chair and goes out to the garden, where she stands and gazes into the forest for a long time, her hands uncharacteristically idle.

CHAPTER 5

Caden spends the next couple of days in town asking among the traders and a few other Rangers in the area. One or two have heard of the missing Fae, but there's no new information. Nor does he have any luck tracking down the drunken hermit. It's getting colder, and that strange urge to go and look for Sislie is getting stronger. It feels like it's his destiny. He doesn't waste more time looking for nonexistent clues.

The evening before he leaves, Moriko goes to the pantry and opens a tiny cupboard he's never noticed before. He watches, puzzled, as she takes out a small clay flask with a cork stopper. She pulls a tiny cloth envelope from her tool drawer and pours a thimbleful of grey powder into it.

"This will help your seeking-sight. Put a pinch of it in hot water tonight and let it steep for a few minutes. Drink it before you go to sleep. Then later, while you're out questing, if you have gone two full days with no clue, do it again. Remember, more won't help. If you take too much or too often, it will just befuddle your senses and might make you sick."

His eyes widen at his mother, again revealing more about herself.

“It's from your grandfather, from across the sea. My father gave it to me. It's a wonderful gift, but comes at a price, so don't overuse it.”

That night, he dreams of the Fae dancer. *She's laughing, violet eyes sparkling in a heart-shaped face. A bright glow surrounds her. She twirls in a forest glade, gossamer wings unfurled.* She becomes more substantial as he watches in the dream. He is transfixed. Her golden curls draw him in to their frothy effervescence. Sislie, it must be Sislie. He falls into a deep sleep.

“Did you see?” His mother brings morning tea to his bed, and a glass of water.

He nods, groggy. “She's...”

“Sh-sh, don't talk, just remember.” She leaves him to his memory, a glowing image of beauty like nothing he's ever seen. Delicate Fae features floating in a golden cloud. Violet eyes he could sink into without fear of drowning.

Caden fills his carrysack with essentials for the search, still absorbed in reverie. Absently, he tucks his wooden flute into his pocket, and fastens his rolled-up blanket to the loops which Moriko has attached at the bottom for this purpose. He adds newly fletched arrows to his quiver, including a couple that have the valuable metal tips best for large game, which could also penetrate leather armor if needed. He's not expecting trouble, but just in case.

His mother adds a bundle of fresh bread and cheese, and the delicious forest cakes full of nuts and dried fruit that last a long time and provide a tasty addition to small game and berries, which are becoming scarce as the cold weather approaches. He also knows how to forage for nuts, edible mushrooms and roots. He doesn't carry a cooking pot, but can fashion one out of birch bark if he starts to hunger for a stew instead of the usual raw or roasted travel fare.

When he's ready to go, he hugs his mother and smiles down at her. "Don't worry about me, I'll be fine and I'll bring you a handsome reward."

Moriko gazes into her son's eyes, her deep brown eyes meeting his with blessing for a successful venture and safe return. She starts to say something, but then lowers her gaze and it remains unspoken.

He hoicks the packsack onto his back and carefully fastens his bow in a sling. His mother gave him the bow as a gift last fall, when he became a full Ranger, never saying where it came from. Caden thinks it's enchanted, crafted by the reclusive elves who don't trade with just anyone. He's always been a very good marksman, since their neighbor Jacob made him a little bow when he was small, and taught him to shoot tiny arrows at a target mounted on a bale of hay. But since he got this bow, his aim has gone from excellent to near perfect. His mother always evaded his questions about where it came from, though he thought traders were unlikely to have brought it. And the standoffish Fae? Even less likely.

His trail to Cougar Mountain passes through the town. It's market day, so he makes a quick visit to several traders, hoping for more clues. There are only a few vague rumors that he doesn't give much credence.

He heads out, following the upstream trail towards Cougar Mountain where he saw that hut that seems to deflect his gaze. The senior Rangers gave him permission to take one of the horses since this is a rescue mission. So he should be able to get there in a couple of days.

As he turns past the trading post on the way out of town, his path is blocked by a group of stern looking Fae. Not just any group, they look like an entourage for some noble—an ancient female with sharp features, her skin so taut across her cheekbones that she looks almost skeletal beneath her Youthfulness glamour. Her mouth is a thin straight line and her purple, almost black eyes have a piercing look sharper than her features. She sits on a palanquin carried by four servants, and wears an ornate gown unsuitable for travel. Her elaborate green and gold feathered headpiece seems to float and glisten.

Caden quickly assesses the eight attendants. Four are clearly warriors, also one tall fair-haired male beside her, who stands very stiff and gazes away over Caden's head. He could be a warrior, by build and stance, but his embroidered velvet surcoat and finely tooled scabbard, belt and boots establish him as a noble. As Caden examines him, his heart inexplicably skips a beat and his breath catches.

Three females complete the party, standing behind the old woman and ahead of the warriors. Handmaidens, he surmises, giving them a cursory scan. But as he glances at the tallest of the handmaidens, who wears her hair in a crown of braids, they're both startled by a flash of recognition. He wonders where he's seen her before, and a memory pops up, of his mother crafting a delicate turquoise fabric for the—*ohgods*—for the Fae Queen. Could this be her?

Queen Maelys is the ruler of the Land but has never been known to visit First Bend, nor any of the predominantly Human towns and villages that dot its coastlines and river shores. He almost staggers with the realization.

The old woman points at him with two bejeweled fingers. "You, boy. Come here."

CHAPTER 6

"You moron!" He kicks the downed Raider, who shrinks against the wooden rails of the walkway running along the ridge above their village. "You've killed the Fae Queen-to-be. What made you think you could kidnap her for ransom? Whose idiotic notion was that?"

Broad shouldered and muscular, with his bald head, dark almost black eyes, gold earring, and chains around his neck, Chance's rage makes him look just like his pirate father. He's been the leader of the Shorelanders since his father, captain of the original shipwreck, died two years ago.

But Chance is not a pirate. He has negotiated a precarious alliance with the merchants whose ship was also wrecked on their treacherous coast, promising to build a better life for all of them. Since then, he's been scheming to establish trade with the Fae, and get the Rocky Shorelanders into the good graces of their ancient Queen. They desperately need more arable land, because there's none on their side of the peninsula opposite the three mountains and Queensdale Valley. If only they could negotiate a land grant across from First Bend town. And equally important, access to the port downstream.

But these reckless, ungovernable fools have laid it all to waste. Chance kicks him one more time, then motions impatiently to Pokum, his first mate, to return the badly beaten miscreant to their stockade next to the stable. He paces back and forth on the wooden walkway overlooking the meager village square of Rocky Shores. He frantically wracks his brain to come up with some way to get out of this disaster, some ally, some solution, something, anything. His angry scowl and intimidating fists deter anyone from coming near.

Pokum trudges up the stairs from the stockade, carefully maintaining a bland look on his round face, cautious after the tirade. "They didn't know, Chance. They just thought they'd be able to get some ransom money, and maybe have a little fun with her...." The mate is silenced by Chance's black scowl.

"How did they get into the arms locker? Those crossbows are our main defense, not playthings for imbeciles."

"That's one of the worst parts. They bribed the Quartermaster, promising to share their loot and give him a turn with the Fae female. I've already fired him."

Chance has never been so furious. The only reason he hasn't bludgeoned them to death is because Pokum restrained him, at the risk of his own beating, persuading him it would only deepen the divisions between the two factions in their settlement. The merchants have been on his side, and until now he thought he'd be able to bring the factions together. But he can't contain the Raiders, ruffians egged on by the last of the older pirates with their made-up stories about a life of adventure and loot.

Since the death of his father, the Raiders in the pirate faction have become more intractable—increasing their forays into First

Bend and other towns, stealing from the homesteads, robbing merchants at the port, and even kidnapping women, who are scarce in their settlement because the original ships were crewed by men. The Human communities have always been suspicious of them, and wary of the few Shorelanders who have befriended their residents. Even the ones who have married into their families are treated with mistrust.

Chance doesn't know if he can placate the Fae for the death of young Marielle. Blaming the lawless ruffians from the pirate faction may not be enough. He's still desperate to persuade the Fae and their Queen to establish peaceful relations.

He spends the next several days visiting the merchant traders and his allies among the pirates, coaxing them to contribute the remaining tradable goods salvaged from their wrecked ships, promising them the best land holdings once they are granted by the Fae Queen.

Both merchant and pirate ships carried luxury goods such as silks, carpets, spices—cinnamon and ginger—precious stones, gold embroidery, porcelain, mirrors. Most of these were damaged or lost in the shipwrecks, but enough was salvaged that Chance is able to amass enough treasure to fill a couple of chests. He hopes to offer these to the Fae Queen in reparation.

As additional proof of good will and genuine remorse, he'll turn the raiding party over to the Fae, to punish as they see fit.

CHAPTER 7

Lady Nerysa collapses against her husband's chest. The constant fear grinds her belly and tightens the band across her chest, threatening to squeeze off her breathing. It creeps along her spine and insinuates itself around her throat. "My precious Sislie, my daughter, where are you? Why can't I sense you?" The Fae parents, normally serene and distinguished, cling to each other, trying in vain to find some comfort in the midst of the unthinkable.

"Torin, she can't be dead. I know she's not dead." The Lady Nerysa and Lord Torin are both healers, and would have sensed if their daughter had died. They also would have sensed if she was injured. "She must be drugged. That's the only way her essence could be so completely hidden from our seekers, and especially from me."

Lord Torin has just returned from searching Raven's Peak with the Hummingbird Clan warriors. The others have continued on to scour the other two mountains that encircle Queensdale Valley. He paces back and forth in their comfortably furnished drawing room near the edge of the treetop village, oblivious to the splendid view overlooking the forest. "I'm most worried about the Raiders," he frets, "but they fled to the other side of the peninsula after Marielle's murder, and there's no evidence of their having kidnapped her. Or anyone else, either. If someone is holding her for ransom, we should have heard from them by now."

CHAPTER 8

The cottage is in pandemonium. Splinters of my little chair and table are strewn all over, herbs scattered, the gooey brown remains of porridge smeared on the floor beside a broken bowl. And blood. Blood on the floor, on the big table. That rasping sound is Ragana breathing, or snoring—I can't tell. Broken bowls crunch under my feet as I find a candle, and crouch down to check on her, trying to quell the panic and horror. She's lying on the floor, one leg twisted at a bad angle. She looks awful, blood all over her face, and one eye swollen shut.

I jerk back, startled, when she opens her other eye and whispers something I can't hear. She plucks at my sleeve to pull me closer and keeps whispering and groaning until I can tell what she's saying. "Light fire." She doesn't let go of me, and after what feels like a long wait, "Fetch water. Heat. Small pan. Flowers. Top row. Third bundle. Brew handful." She faints, but I can still hear her rasping breath.

I run to do her bidding, used to obeying her. I trip and fall on the way back up from the stream, spilling half the water, but I ignore the sting of my scraped knee and keep going. I use the candle to light some kindling in the fireplace and soon there's enough fire to heat the small pot of water. While it's heating, I wet a rag and wipe the blood from her forehead. For some reason, this has a calming effect on me. The cut is deep enough to see some white of bone, and it's still bleeding, a lot. I cover it with a clean cloth. She groans but doesn't wake up.

By now, the water is boiling and I dump in a handful of the dried flowers she asked for. As it simmers, the brew fills the cottage with the smell of summer. I breathe in the aroma of lavender, apples, peaches, and something else I can't name. After a while, I strain some into her bowl and blow on it to cool it, just like I used to for... someone.

I sit on the floor and cradle her head with one arm. I try to spoon some of the medicine into her mouth, but it just dribbles down the side of her cheek. Then I drizzle a few drops on her lips. She licks it up, her tongue slowly moving across her bottom lip. Then again. And again. She tries to lift her head. She can't do it, but I manage to help her raise her head enough to take a few sips from the spoon.

She rests her head back on my arm and looks up at me with a strange look in her eyes. Now that the panic has subsided, I sit and return her gaze. I realize the look in her eyes is fear. I've been her captive. My gut clenches in revulsion and I slide my arm out from under her head as quickly as I can without hurting her, laying her back on the floor. I stand up and back away from her. I'm disgusted that I've been helping her. I feel angry, ashamed, scared.

I could escape now. I should escape. I don't know where I am and have no idea where I'd escape to, but I need to get out of here. The sleeping powder is wearing off but my head feels like it's packed tight with down feathers. Somewhere I know there's another life and something I'm supposed to do. And I have a name. I must have a name. Silly... Sister... Suh... Suh... I try to catch a memory but the feathers just float away, and my head starts to spin. My throat feels tight. My chest aches.

I want to curl up on my sleeping pallet, but I pull myself together. I ignore the feathers and start looking around for things to escape with. I spot the carrysack near the door. It's full of those flat cakes she was baking. Travel cakes. I take half of them out of the carrysack and wrap them in an apron. The nights are getting cooler, so I rummage around for a cape or blanket I can use to stay warm.

Just as I reach the door, Ragana groans. I stop. I should get away from this cottage and this old woman who drugged me and held me, but something makes me put the travel cakes back into their carrysack and check on her again. I fight against the urge to make her well in spite of my disgust and anger. Am I a healer? Is that why I recognized so many of the herbs on her drying rack? Not knowing why, I kneel at her head and place my hands on either side of her face.

I close my eyes and hold her like this for a moment. My hands *feel* into her head, sensing the hot area around her eye and the cut on her forehead. She has a concussion. That urge to make her well is stronger. My shoulder blades start to tingle. Of course. It's my wing nubs. I know this. I'm Fae. I have wings. They retract into my wing nubs when I'm not using them. The tingling increases, and heat permeates my chest. It's heartfire. A stream of energy surges down my arms. I flow the wellness into her body, and feel the injury begin to heal.

Her head is going to be ok, but she has a broken leg. I'm suddenly too exhausted to help her with it, or figure out how, but healing her feels right, normal.

I doze for a while, sitting with her, but wake up with my gut sore and gnawing. Ragana is still asleep, and I cover her with the blanket from her bed. Her breathing is deeper now. A chilly dawn is sliding in past the broken door, which means I haven't eaten since yesterday morning. I inspect the stewpot, half full of cold cabbage stew. I shouldn't want any because it was always drugged, but I'm hungry and there's nothing else to eat. Though she was eating it too, so it must have been my bowl that got the sleeping powder. I sniff it first, inspecting for the smell of the herb that always seemed to be in my food. I take a chance and gobble down two bowlfuls. I'm more awake than I've ever been in this cottage but still full of confusion. Feathers.

By now it's light outside, and she's awake. "More," she croaks.

I give her most of what's left of the potion.

"Thank you" her voice still weak and raspy. "Pour some brew on a clean rag and put it on my eye."

I fold the wet cloth several times and place it on her swollen eye.

She gasps, but puts her hand over it to hold it there. "How big is the cut?"

I indicate the length of my baby finger.

"Under the table," she rasps, "smallest basket. Curved needle, thread. Sew it shut."

I fetch the needle and thread, and pour more of the brew over her forehead. The cut is close to the hairline. I take one tiny stitch at a time. Sewing skin is weird. It pulls and stretches with every suture. I keep feeling like this isn't the right way to heal a wound, but I can't think of any other way. The thought tickles something in my brain, but when I try to grasp it, the feathers float away again.

She doesn't flinch as I stitch eight small sutures across her forehead. When I'm done, I pour the last of the brew over the wound and wrap it with a clean rag. I change the cloth over her eye. She sleeps again, sometimes groaning or muttering something I can't make out.

I take a look at her twisted leg, gently lifting her skirt. Her foot looks ok, but it's resting with the inside of her ankle on the floor and her bony knee is purple and swollen. I *feel* the leg. The knee is sprained, and the shinbone has a minor fracture I can splint and help it heal. I pick up a broken leg from the little table that used to sit near the door, and bring it over for a splint. Then I try to gently ease the foot, to straighten it out. She cries out in pain and shock, making me drop it.

"What are you doing!" her voice is stronger now. "Oh, my knee. How bad does it look?"

I describe the distended and purple joint and fractured shin bone, and how her foot is lying on its inside ankle.

"Lift the knee, not the ankle. Sit beside it. No, other side. Close as you can. Gently but quick. If I scream, pay no mind. Then take my heel and straighten out the leg."

I follow her instructions. It's now clear that I'm a healer and probably know better than she does, but there's so much I can't remember. But as I take up her knee, I'm feeling that calm again, and the heat in my chest. I wait for the scream, but it's only a loud groan. I hold her knee close to my chest and use my foot to straighten her leg by pushing the heel away. She moans and cries, but tells me to keep going. Once her leg is almost straight, I fasten the splint along the outside of her calf with strips of cloth, then we manage to get her up on her big chair. I prop her leg on the stool with a cushion under her knee to keep the pressure off.

I rekindle the fire and fetch more water for the healing potion. A thought feather drifts in my mind, that I should have some too. I'm not injured, so I try to grasp for the reason, but the feathers fly and make my head spin again. I pour some into a cup and breathe in the aroma. I take a sip, then another. The taste of summer suffuses my body like a warm breeze, blowing out the effects of the sleeping power and its debilitating lethargy.

As it fills me, I feel stronger, energized, exhilarated. I burst out laughing. I almost feel like me again. Whoever that is doesn't matter right now. I do a little pirouette and dance around the middle of the floor, hugging myself.

When I stop, I look around at this little cottage where I've spent so much time sleeping on that pallet near the low end of the roof, tormented by confused and angry dreams I don't understand. That elusive something I'm supposed to do is feeling urgent, and frustration takes over, dampening my good mood.

I hear her stirring, and light another candle because it's dark again except for the light from the fireplace. I carry it to Ragana. Her eye's still swollen shut, but the swelling has gone down.

"Put a new cloth with the brew on my eye," she rasps, "and another one on my knee."

I wet new rags and pour several drops directly into the cut. I give her more to drink. And take another few sips myself. The surge of well-being almost overwhelms me. But then, something new. I have... feelings. I'm still scared and mad, but now I'm also hopeful. Curious. Maybe even strong. I haven't always been a captive, definitely not her slave. I remember that worried look she gave me when I fed her the potion. She was scared. Afraid I'll abandon her, helpless and injured. I could, if I knew where to go. But something inside me knows it would be wrong. I hate her, but I should help her. It's contradictory and I try to think about it, but the feathers fly and I have to fight the dizziness that makes the room spin.

"Ragana, would you like some food? I'll put more cabbage in the stew and fetch some vegetables from the garden."

"My name's not Ragana. It's Gundega, or at least that's the name they gave me."

They gave her? Who gave her? Eyes wide, I look at her. It's the first time she's said anything to me that wasn't a command.

"Yes please," she says, "I'm hungry. You can add some herbs from the fourth row. You choose, for flavor." She pauses for a breath. "I wasn't always like this, you know. Before they took me, I was more like you, young, shining, inquisitive."

Before they... what? Who? Like me? Questions tumble around my head, a flurry of dispersing thought feathers. I open my mouth to ask.

"Later," not so raspy this time. "First, we eat."

The questions pursue me outside on my way to the garden. *Wait a minute. They were looking for me. That's why they beat up Ragana, um, Gundega.* They cartwheel in my brain. *Who are they? What do they want with me? Who am I? Did she kidnap me? Why? What's going on?* I'm overwhelmed with confusion and panic. I can't breathe. I lean against the side of the cottage, sliding down the wall until I'm sitting on the ground. I gasp for air. The gasps become sobs as I hug my knees and weep on the chilly ground, feeling like it will never stop.

When I'm done, I get up, knees shaking. I go to look in the garden. There's no moonlight, but I can see pretty well. I dig up a rutabaga and some carrots. There's still some water in one of the pails, so I wash them by the cottage instead of going down to the stream. I notice my cupboard door is slightly open and push it closed. Back inside, I start to chop the vegetables. The rhythm of chopping quiets my racing mind and disjointed pictures float around—*a clearing.... a village in the trees... a pesky little girl... a glow surrounds me... luminous wings....*

I don't know what any of it means, but tears are leaking out of my eyes and fall on the vegetables. My chest and throat ache with despair and longing. These must be people and places I know, maybe where I live. I see a Fae Lady. *She laughs as she tosses someone high in the air, spinning. There's a small child giggling. It's me.* Could she be my mother?

I look at the old woman sleeping. I'm not going to leave her, and I can't think of anything else to do, so I return to the vegetables and the stew pot, adding a couple of herbs for flavor. As the stew simmers, I heat more water for the healing herbs, adding another from the top row, that I recognize is for pain.

Gundega's awake again, giving me that same worried look. I bring her more of the potion. She sips some, frowns, but then says "Oh, ok, for pain. Thank you." She's able to sit up and sip on her own. I bring her a bowl of stew, and one for myself. She eats it all, then I help her to her sleeping pallet and cover her with her blanket. My thoughts are too churned up to let me sleep, so I sweep up the broken pottery and bundle the sticks of furniture into kindling. I do a clumsy repair on the door, so at least it will close.

I grab the water buckets and slowly follow the curving path down to the stream, noticing again that I can see even though there's not much moonlight. When I get there, I put down the buckets and wade into the water. It's cold, but I sink down and let it wash over me. I'm shivering, but the water carries away the staleness of confinement, and more of the exhaustion from the sleeping power I've had so much of. I'm chilled but energized, and for the first time, I'm not the least bit drowsy.

I fill the buckets and take them back to the cottage. I build up the fire, and stand close, to dry my hair and the worn shift I've been wearing. The sparks from the fire are dancing, and I start to sway and turn, first slowly, then faster, as a song floats on the air.

It's me. I'm singing. My arm reaches forward of its own accord and the other reaches backward, toward my extended leg. I move through several poses. They have a practiced feel, and words drift through my head. *Plié, arabesque*. I don't know what they mean, but they feel good, sound good.

Soon I'm dry, and sleepy. Almost cozy. I still feel the achy sadness, but it's smoother, calmer. I fetch my sleeping pallet from the secret cupboard and lie down for the first normal sleep I've had since I've been in Gundega's cottage.

In the morning, she is up before me, hobbling around with her walking stick. "Here, have some porridge." She places a bowl on the table and gestures for me to join her there.

I hesitate, remembering the horrible lethargy of sleeping powder.

"It's ok, there's no sleeping powder in it." She takes a spoonful from the bowl she offered me. "Serve yourself from the pot if you don't believe me." I trust her this time, and accept the bowl.

We eat, then, "Look" she unties the lace from her shirt and pulls it off her right shoulder. There's something colored brown and gray on her shoulder. It's got a faint sheen, but blurry, and there's a scar running through it. I look more closely and gasp. I know this symbol. It looks like a Fae sigil, the mark we all have, unique to each Clan. But she's an old Human. Why does she have a Lynx Clan sigil on her shoulder?

CHAPTER 9

Gundega settles into her big chair and adjusts her foot on the stool. She points to the door with her walking stick. "When they come back to look for you again, grab that carry-sack and run. Follow the slope downhill, and you'll come to a trail that goes all the way down to Queensdale."

"Who are they? What do they want with me? Who is that 'she'? And why do you have the Lynx Clan sigil?" Questions pile up and spill out.

Her eyes shift uneasily away from me. "There's lots to tell, but I'm not going anywhere with this broken leg. I'll start with the sigil."

I move my chair to the other side of the fireplace. I want to know about the ruffians, but she refuses to talk about them, so I try to settle down and listen to her story.

"They took me when I was too young to remember. There were two of us. The other girl was Mina. She was a bit older than me and had the squirrel Clan sigil. She had been there a while. I was just old enough to talk, and Mina remembered enough of our language that we developed a kind of lingo made up of Fae and the Human tongue combined. The woman taking care of us didn't like us talking like that because she couldn't understand Fae and we talked too fast. But she was kind enough in her way. She used to take us into the forest to look for mushrooms and plants that could be used for medicine or food. She had a bit of magic, and taught us herbs and how to heal wounds.

"The village was primitive. Most of them lived in crude huts with walls made of rough woven mats. They called themselves the Asmung. The men of the village were often away, hunting or raiding for food or skins or other things to trade. They were not successful traders, because they would steal and the other villages and tribes didn't trust them. Also, they were unkempt and had a peculiar odor.

"There were few children, and many of those were weak and sickly. She mostly kept us away from them, which was fine because they'd laugh at us and throw things. Later, they were afraid of us, but that was after we made up simple spells to make them trip or stumble into each other. When we got older, the woman gave us more responsibility for preparing food and treating ailments."

She shifts and groans in her chair, readjusting her injured leg on the stool. "Mina and I were often taken to the women's lodge. She made us rub their bellies and genitals. They believed we had healing power for the infertile women. This ended one spring when Mina had her first blood.

"After that I was still taken to the women's tent, but when I came back, she'd be gone, later to stumble or be carried back, bruised and bleeding between her legs even if it wasn't her moon time. She wouldn't talk about it, but I soon figured out they were trying to breed her with the tribe's headman, Brom, because none of his women had been able to conceive. After an unfruitful year of this, he cast her off to his youngest brother, who had no woman."

I'm almost jumping out of my chair "but Raga, um, Gundega, why didn't you run away?"

Gundega's voice is sounding more like her normal croak. "I was just a child, and I didn't remember any other life.

"I didn't see much of Mina after that. But later that year, she showed signs that she was with child. The baby grew enormous in her small body and as the time came close, she struggled to walk, even trying to carry her enormous belly in her arms.

"The Human baby was too big for her. It survived the birth, but they left her spent and bleeding in the women's tent. They didn't care about her, just the baby. After, I dragged her body out to a rocky place and covered it with stones, piled as high as I could. She was my only friend, and I never had another.

"That night I stole a small knife and as much food as I could carry, and ran. I had no idea where I was going, but I knew which way the hunters usually went, so I went the other way. I ran all night and the next day. I followed rabbit and fox trails and ate what was left of the berries because winter was coming. I ran until I couldn't stand any more and then I hid in a tree, in the fork of two large branches. I tied myself to one of them so I wouldn't fall out.

"I ran all that fall and winter, and the next spring. I ran all the way down the mountain and across the valley between. I mostly followed animal trails. The Human trails were wider and easier, so sometimes I followed them, but I hid if I saw anyone.

"When it got cold, I stole a blanket that kept me from freezing, and enough food to keep me alive, but just barely. When I could, I slept in barns, where the sheep kept me warm. I was terrified of everything, and I think I went insane. Sometimes I passed a Fae village. I could see it because I was Fae, and maybe I should have recognized it as a safe place. But after what happened to Mina, I was too afraid. I kept myself hidden, and they either didn't notice me or just gave me my privacy, not recognizing my distress.

"Finally, in early summer, I came to this creek just below us. I found a battered old pot left by travelers, and some wild cabbages. I had some cooking skills from the Asmung woman, and I made a cabbage stew, the best meal I have ever eaten. The cottage was falling down. I fixed it up.

"Over the years, I spied on Fae children from a village not too far from here, and I learned some of their glamours. I learned the glamour of Unnoticeability, that makes things blend into their surroundings. That keeps the cottage away from the gaze of hunters and passers-by."

"But your sigil, it's broken. How can this be? What happened to it? They can't break." *How do I know this?* "And why do you look like an old Human woman and not like a Fae?"

"While I was running, I came into my moon time. But I was starving and my wing nubs never matured. Then, by the time I settled into this place and had enough to eat, they were shriveled. Maybe if I had someone to heal me, it would have been different. But there wasn't. So, I am Fae, but not. The sigil gradually faded and as I grew, it split and scarred. I'm not really that much older than you, but I became old very quickly. I don't know why. So, I'm not like you, not Fae, but not Human either."

She stops, listening, and glances at the door.

I get up and bolt for the carrysack by the door. "Wait," she holds up her hand.

We hear rustling and chittering of small animals in the forest, but too many of them, and the sound is growing. Then breaking branches and stomping hooves of animals, ignoring their usual paths. Some growls and cries, but mostly it sounds like a storm.

Then we smell the smoke.

CHAPTER 10

Minason smiles to himself. He can almost taste the rabbit he's about to snag. He kneels at the opening to its burrow, his quick hands perfectly still, waiting for it to show more than a quivering nose.

Up here at the top of Dragon's End Mountain, this is a meal he can roast and savor by himself. Almost full grown, he's always hungry. Especially when his greedy Da shoves him aside and leaves him nothing in the pot but bones and gristle. He'll save the skin for Sula, for a cozy muff to keep her hands warm in winter.

The rabbit ventures a half step out of its burrow and quick as a cat, he scoops it up. But something glistens at him from under a brambleberry bush and, distracted, he loosens his grip. The lucky rabbit wriggles free and scampers.

Ignoring the brambles, Minason parts the branches to see what's there. He pulls out a big river rock, almost as big as the rabbit, but surprisingly light. Turquoise blazes zigzag around the middle and spiral to the ends. It's beautiful. His best find ever. He hugs the prize in his thin arms, hopping like he does when there's nobody looking.

Hunger forgotten, he returns to inspect the brambleberry bush that hid his treasure. He pulls out another three stones, almost like the first, brightly streaked with silver and turquoise blazes. He sits and cradles the beautiful prizes in his lap, rocking and crooning to them. The streaks shimmer more brightly as he holds them. Maybe they're magic.

Minason loves his mountain top. It's scrubby and rocky, but nobody else comes here. Nobody calls him fairy or taunts him for being tall and thin and light of skin, or for his pale violet eyes. And the steam vent keeps his cave warm even in the winter.

Here he can dream. He imagines himself flying, drifting on air currents the way the ravens do. And he moons over Sula. Her shiny black pebble eyes, and the endearing gap between her front teeth. And the time she hugged him when he gave her a rabbit. But her father beat him afterwards and told him to stay away. They kept the rabbit, though.

The other youth of the Asmung village used to taunt him and throw sticks, and wreck his drawings, but now they mostly ignore him. He likes that. He can forage undisturbed at the old midden for scraps of pottery and wood for his drawings, and won't later find them stomped or pissed on. But even though he's sure they won't come looking, he always hides his possessions in the shallow cave at the edge of the steam vent.

Looking around carefully to make sure there's no one to see him, he carries the four rocks to his cave, pushing them behind his drawings and scraps. Maybe tomorrow he can talk Sula into coming to see his new treasures. She says his drawings are stupid, but the stones are shiny and she might like them.

It's getting dark. Minason goes back to the rabbit burrow and waits patiently until he can snatch another rabbit. He trots down the path to the hut he shares with his Da, who is waiting for him at the door of their shabby dwelling, a familiar scowl on his face. He cuffs him and scolds him for being late with his supper. Minason is not really late, but Da often hits him for no good reason, and sometimes beats him when he's in a temper over something else.

That night the mountain shakes. Minason is startled awake, his straw filled sleeping pallet bouncing and shuddering. Disoriented, he first thinks it's his Da snoring, but it's too loud. The dirt floor is shaking too. Confused, he crawls to the doorway of their hut, reaching it just as the shaking stops. He peers outside.

"Help me! Help! Save me!" Screaming villagers are bursting out of their shacks, afraid and confused. They mill around the square.

"What's happening?"

An old woman shrieks, "It's the dragons—they're back, that's them roaring! They'll burn our village! Run!"

"Mamma, Mamma, help me! Help!" the two young men who taunt him the worst are crying and clinging to their mothers.

Then the shaking starts again, even harder, knocking villagers off their feet. Its grating clamour hurts his ears. With a loud explosion a tree falls, demolishing several huts at the end of the village. After a few minutes, the shaking stops and there's a moment of silence, as the entire village takes a collective breath. Then the wailing resumes.

Afterward, his Da is one of the first to go back into his hut. He drinks a cup of the fermented hooch he hides in the back corner of their hut, then settles back down on his sleeping pallet, muttering to himself. Some of the villagers are huddled outside their doors, afraid their huts will fall on them in their sleep. The rest gradually fade back into their shacks, fearful but safe for the moment. The air has a sulfurous smell.

He eventually returns to his own sleeping pallet, but Minason can't settle down. He's worried about his treasures. He waits until he hears his Da turn over and fart, then snore again. Then he steals out of the hut. He hurries up the animal trails, glad of his keen night vision. The many downed trees block his way, forcing him to clamber over them in the dark. He almost stumbles into a large crevasse which makes him skirt far out of his way. Tomorrow he'll use one of the fallen trees to make a bridge across it, but now he races to the summit, desperate to find his magic rocks.

At the top, breathless, his jaw drops and he can only stare. Then he howls in dismay. The cave is gone, devoured by the steam vent, which is now a wide fissure full of hot reddish smoke. He falls to his knees and crawls as close as he can, to inspect the ruin of his cave. Most of his precious drawings are gone, consumed by the inferno below. Worse yet, one of his new treasures has also vanished. The remaining three stones are perched on a narrow ledge on the remaining wall of what's left of his cave. It's too hot and too far for him to reach.

"No, No, No!" Hot tears mingle with the sweat running down his cheeks as he vainly searches the rest of the plateau, shouting and crying.

Finally, spent, throat aching, he returns to the edge of his ruined cave. He looks more closely at the rocks. Through the smoke, the turquoise streaks are brighter and one of them is pulsating. He sits down to watch them, as close as he can without burning himself. Gradually, fascination overrules dismay and the mesmerizing pulse draws him into his usual daydream. He imagines himself flying. He soars, and rides the high winds as he's watched the falcons and ravens do. Eventually he curls up on the ground near the crevasse and sleeps.

In the morning he dodges his Da's slap. "Get my breakfast, you lazy slug, then get out there and help your Baba. Her roof got damaged last night." His Da stomps to the table, plopping his squat body onto the stool to wait for his food. His dark hair falls over his brow, meeting a perpetual scowl. He is short and thick, like most of the villagers, in contrast to his tall son, whose long pale arms and legs accentuate his thin frame and have made him the target of a lifetime of taunts and bullying, the worst being from his own father.

Later, his uncle, the headman Brom, orders all the young people to clean up the village square. Most of the huts are still standing, but many of them are damaged. It takes all day and the next because the other youth, who are supposed to be cleaning up too, spend most of their time taunting pelting him with debris from the earthshake.

It's several days before he can make his way back to his treasures. On the way up the mountain, he drags a couple of small tree trunks and fashions a crude bridge across the crevasse that had blocked his way the night of the earthshake. When he gets to the top, the stones are still there, still glowing through the reddish smoke. But they're too far to reach, and it's too hot. There's no way to retrieve them.

He can't make it up every day, but whenever he can, he sits cross-legged for hours, gazing at his glowing rocks, rocking and crooning to them, lost in his daydreams or making drawings of the pulsating stones perched at the edge of the abyss. Until the day one of the stones trembles. Startled, he looks around. The earth didn't shake again, or did it? The stone trembles again and starts to rock.

"Oh no! It's going to fall in." He grabs the largest slab of wood from his drawing supplies and slides it onto the ledge. Taking a deep breath, he shimmies onto the board and reaches as far as he can, trying to ignore the scorching on his belly and arms. He inches forward, the hot pain almost unbearable, but then the tip of his finger brushes against the trembling stone. He almost topples it, but manages to hook one end and roll it towards himself without knocking it into the hot fissure barely an inch away. He shimmies back off the ledge until he can bring it away, nesting it carefully between some rocks so that it won't roll away.

Just as he starts to breathe again, another stone trembles. Gasping in pain from his burns, he returns to the scorched board and retrieves the second stone, placing it carefully on the ground next to the first one. And then the third. Then he stumbles to his carrysack and water skin, to pour water onto his blistering belly and arms. His ruined shirt will earn him a beating, and the pain is incredible, but even sobbing, he shouts in triumph, "I saved them! I saved them." He hops and dances, brimming with joy and pain in equal measure.

His eyes rest for a fond moment on his precious stones. Where can he hide them? The village has never been safe. Too many thieving eyes and jeering voices. Maybe in that abandoned rabbit warren over the ridge.

Now two stones are trembling, but the first one is rocking harder, and horrified, he watches it start to roll down the slope, picking up speed as it goes. He jumps up, pain forgotten, and chases it, flapping his skinny arms, shrieking and crying, panicked to see it tumble over a ledge and crash down onto a wide shelf below with a loud crack. He hurtles over the ledge, reckless of his own safety. The stone is cracked, the turquoise streaks no longer pulsating. Then he gapes dumbfounded as the stone rocks more violently and cracks wide open.

Gods! It's an egg. A scrawny turquoise bird wrestles its ungainly way out of the shell, snorting and hissing as it finds its feet, long wings flopping on the ground. Instead of feathers, it's covered in fish scales, shining faintly, the same color as the turquoise streaks on the egg. Its beak looks like a tiny snout.

Minason reaches to pick it up, but he hears the second egg rolling down the hill. He can't stop it, but dives and manages to steer it toward the ledge where the first egg tumbled over.

It also crashes and cracks open, to reveal another scrawny bird, which tussles its way out of the broken shell. By now the first bird has spread its wings, which drag on the ground as it staggers around, tiny claws clicking on the smooth stone surface. It hisses and snorts at the second bird, and shambles close to the edge.

Minason scoops it up with both hands so it won't fall off the ledge. It's about the size of a rabbit, except for its floppy wings, which hang down over both sides of his hands. Its scaly skin is smooth and warm. It tries to wriggle out of his hands, but he contains it easily as he runs up to another cave on the far side of the clearing, where he stores extra pieces of wood and clay. He tucks the bird into the cave and drags some branches across its opening to keep the flightless bird inside, then scurries down to where the second bird is just beginning to stagger around. He grabs it as well, and places it in the cave with the first bird. Then he goes to check on the third, and smallest, egg. It's trembling and rocking, but only slightly. Safe to leave it for a little while.

He takes a hard biscuit from his carrysack and carefully breaks it into three pieces. He takes two of them and places them cautiously in front of the birds. They snort and hiss, turning away from the food. He's hungry himself, and thoughtfully chews on the dry and almost tasteless biscuit, wondering what to feed these peculiar birds. They're definitely not some kind of chicken. Chickens would peck at the biscuits. *But they have no beaks. Would they eat insects?* Grubs?

Just then a mouse scurries across the cave and both birds pounce at it, clumsily missing.

Aha, predators, he realizes, and, first checking on the third egg, which is still rocking but only slightly, he dashes to the alpine meadow, where there will be lots of mice. He readily finds a nest and patiently holds his quick hands at its opening. As soon as the first mouse appears, he scoops it up, then two more. He briskly twists their necks to end their tiny lives before bringing two of them to the hungry birds. They sniff the little carcasses and swallow them whole, then abruptly drop down on the floor of the cave and fall asleep, wings sprawled at their sides.

To his dismay, the third egg is not rocking any more. It shudders, then stops. The pulsating turquoise streaks are fading. *It needs help.* He throws it down on the rock ledge where the other two birds hatched. The egg cracks, and Minason uses a stick to pry it open. He gently pulls out another wondrous bird, not caring that it's ungainly, even ugly, only wishing for it to be well. Cradled in his hands, it struggles for a moment, utters a tiny hiss, and dies.

Fighting tears, he places it gently on the ground and looks around for somewhere he can bury the creature. Suddenly, a raven plunges from the sky, and with a loud squawk snatches the baby from the ledge. It flies over the molten fissure and drops the tiny carcass into the smoke and lava below. The raven circles the clearing twice, squawks again, and flies off.

Minason rushes to the fissure, but the bird is gone. All he can see is the reddish smoke and deep down, a glimpse of dull glowing red. He stands and stares for a moment, burning pain on his belly and a sulfurous taste of smoke on his tongue. But he's still excited and curious about the birds.

He checks on them again. They're stirring and hissing in their sleep. He collects two more mice for each of them, from the traps he left behind, and leaves the little carcasses in their cave before he hurries back down to the village. He hopes his Baba will have some salve for the blistered skin on his belly, and he won't get another beating from his Da.

CHAPTER 11

The Royal Consort stands frozen beside his Queen, in the middle of the bustling path leading out of First Bend. It's market day and the passers-by are carrying baskets of aromatic bread, eggs, cloth, buckets or harnesses, and other goods from the merchants. They have scarcely enough room to get past her palanquin with its surrounding entourage. Nobody stops to stare at the Fae, not even a couple of small children whose mother scurries them away, their unanswered questions echoing in the forest.

He looks at his son. He's watched him in secret for years, as he grew from an inquisitive and mischievous boy to this capable young Ranger dismounting from his horse and walking toward the royal entourage, his packsack and bow on his back, quiver full of arrows placed for easy access. Caden has the amber skin and upward curving eyes of his mother, Moriko. But he shares the straight nose, narrow jaw and deep violet eyes that announce his Fae heritage. Also, the tall stature of his unknown father, himself, Lord Kairon of the Hummingbird Clan. This is the first time they have ever met face to face. Heart bursting with hidden pride, he tries to keep his eyes neutral, looking away, anywhere but at Caden as he pulls up his horse before them. As Royal Consort, he would not be much interested in a half-Fae villager.

Queen Maelys leans forward on her palanquin, briefly revealing jewel encrusted slippers as incongruous on the village path as the crimson silken gown and elaborate green and gold feathered headpiece she wears. She waves back the four warriors who move to protect her from a stranger. She points two bejeweled fingers at Caden. "You, boy. Come here."

Lord Kairon watches his son dismount, face neutral, calculating whether to come as summoned, kneel, or stand in place as though he doesn't know who she is. Kairon hopes he'll make the right choice. The Queen has been more ill-tempered than usual lately. Caden takes a step forward and slowly kneels in the middle of the path, face expressionless.

"Kairon, do you know this young man?" The queen's voice is as sharp as her features.

"I've never met him, sublime Majesty." Factually true, though not entirely accurate. He glances at his son but remains impassive. Their eyes meet for just a moment and something passes between them, the young man's bland expression replaced by a fleeting trace of confusion.

She looks the young man over. "You may stand. Come forward. That's a fine bow you carry. Where did you get it?"

"It was a gift from my mother, your Majesty. For my initiation as a Ranger."

Queen Maelys turns to Kairon, her eyes taking on a sly glint. "His mother is that weaver with a foreign look. He's obviously the by-blow of some vagrant Fae. Ned tells me he's the best seeker among the Rangers."

Turning back to Caden, "Who is your father?" Not waiting for an answer, "Never mind, that's not important now. But how does an ignorant village woman come by an elven-crafted bow? They are rare and much sought after among the Fae. I haven't seen such a one for a very long time." Her eyes narrow. "Show it to me." When he takes half a step back and hesitates, she snaps, "I won't touch it."

He reluctantly pulls out the bow, schooling his face to stay neutral at the casual insult to his mother. It has an almost imperceptible glow, and a tiny rune carved into its tip. He holds it out for her inspection, then replaces it carefully in the sling on his back.

"How would she come by a Fae warrior's bow?" She muses out loud, turning to her consort, "Kairon, didn't you used to have a bow such as this?"

"I did, Splendid One, and still do." He reaches back and touches the tip of his own bow, where an almost imperceptible rune matches the one on his son's.

"And where did you..." but turns her imperious gaze back to Caden, "Never mind. I have a commission for you."

Kairon watches as his son looks like he's about to demur, but then he listens in silence as the Queen continues in her piercing voice.

"A female Fae is missing. You have a reputation as a seeker. You are to find her. She is tall and slender, fully fledged, unusual looking, with curly blonde hair. This is urgent. You are to drop whatever else you're doing and bring her back to me. You will be well rewarded."

Caden goes to say something, but she overrides him. “She has the hummingbird sigil on her shoulder. It’s a Clan symbol that looks much like a tattoo. That’s all you need to know. Her name is Sislie.”

Kairon sees Caden’s reaction to the name. *He already knows about Sislie. He must have heard about the Clan's search and reward for her safe return*. He hastily signals to his son in the hand language of the Rangers. “Pretend to accept her offer. Leave quietly and quickly.” He grits his teeth as Caden looks puzzled for a moment, but then composes his face back to the neutral look.

Oblivious to the reactions of those around her, the Queen snaps at her attendant. “Don't just gape like a fool, Liana, give him the pouch of coins and travel food.”

A tall handmaiden with a crown of braids offers him a generous pouch made of purple brocade and hands it to him. She stares at him but says nothing.

Then the Queen of the Fae reaches into the skirt of her gown. “You will give Sislie this powder in some tea when you find her. It will keep her docile and compliant.”

She doesn't notice him shudder as he accepts the small silken pouch containing the powder, nor the way he brushes off the spell of Compliance she casually casts on him as she turns back to her palanquin.

“You will make all haste. Look first on Cougar Mountain. You’ll bring her to me and only me.”

Kairon signals the servants to lift the palanquin and raises both hands. He draws an elaborate pattern with many angles in the air and speaks buzzing words that swarm around Caden’s ears. A portal opens and for a moment, the forest is silent.

The Queen and her entourage turn as one, step through, and vanish in a single instant. One of the passing villagers cries out in amazement and a small child drops her raisin bun and starts to bawl.

Caden gazes, uneasy, at the spot where the Queen and her entourage disappeared as though they never were. He has seen Fae dancers *flicker* in and out of sight, but never the portal of a group of Fae like this.

He shudders. Queen Maelys has left him with a repulsive crawling feeling, as though insects were swarming on his skin. He brushes himself off. His day started with his heart overflowing with attraction and an eager quest as he set out to find the enchanting Sislie who glowed and smiled in his dream. But now he's full of foreboding. He remembers overhearing worried talk among the older Rangers about the Queen. They alluded to greed and duplicity at court, with only a few at Queensdale working to keep the Queendom safe and functioning. But he never paid much attention to the remote workings of the royal court, more interested in the mountains and forests, hunting, and keeping his eye out for evidence of Raiders.

He saw through her Youthfulness glamour right away. His mother's friend Analena, also half Fae, had taught him to slightly defocus his eyes to see through illusion glamours, and how to deflect other spells if he's ready for them. Once the Queen beckoned to him, he went on alert. She might have looked young and beautiful to the unwary, but she couldn't hide the predatory look in her eye. So he was ready, and the compulsion to obey rolled off him. She didn't even notice. Though that tall handmaiden, Liana, was watching him and saw how he evaded it.

He muses about the courtier. Elegant in his embroidered velvet doublet the color of deep forest, addressing the Queen as Sublime, and Splendid. But he knew the Rangers' hand signals. He must be a trusted ally, if someone taught him their private language for use in the presence of someone they don't trust. And his velvet garb doesn't hide his muscular warrior's build or alert stance. But there's something disquieting about him, that spark that felt like recognition when their eyes met. Caden thinks he'd remember if he had ever seen him before.

He sets that thought aside and tries to cast off the dread, forming a sincere wish that he will never encounter the Queen or her retinue again. But why would the Queen be interested in a young Fae dancer? Vincent said she had some special status, but didn't know what.

He scrutinizes the path he was about to take when he set out. Cougar Mountain. That's where he was headed anyway. If the Queen was urging him to go there, she might have a clue that Sislie could be found there. He doesn't want to let his aversion deflect him from his quest, so he mounts his waiting horse and starts out. He pictures the cottage he saw, disguised as a tumble-down hut. It's a couple of days' riding to get there. He moves off the village path, following the trails and shortcuts he knows as a Ranger, heading toward the mountain.

CHAPTER 12

The royal entourage speedily portals through the low pass and across the river valley to bring Her Glorious Highness back to the palace. They stop for a rest on a wide plateau overlooking Queensdale valley. The air is still warm on the skin, and the last meadow flowers boldly flaunt their autumn reds and yellows. The Queen's handmaidens lay out hibiscus mead and sweet cakes from the baskets they have carried all day, but there is to be no enjoyment during this respite. Queen Maelys has been querulous and impatient, complaining the while that they're going too slowly and completely disregarding her comfort.

Lord Kairon is still shaken after meeting his son face to face for the first time, but stands unmoving beside her palanquin, looking out over the valley. He's anxious he might inadvertently reveal his link to the confident young Ranger with enough presence of mind and skill to deflect the enchantments of the Queen of the Fae.

He closes his eyes for a moment and pictures Caden's mother, his beloved Moriko, her long black hair falling forward over her shoulders. The last time he saw her, it was showing a few strands of silver. He sighs. Their visits have been too few and too far between. He aches for her, her warm eyes, her generous lips, her arms. But he must keep her safe. And his duty to the Queendom must come first. Always his duty.

He sighs again, wishing they could be on their way, absently giving half an ear to his monarch's litany of grievances. He can hardly believe that he once had affection for her, brokenhearted after her previous Consort died so tragically. But then her role in the tragedy was gradually revealed, and his fondness changed into revulsion. Then, over time, her concern for the wellbeing of the Queendom was replaced by avarice. After that, keeping her from despoiling the Land became his primary concern.

She turns her attention to him, her sharp voice piercing his distraction. "Who do you know in that village? Never mind, it's not important. That boy, that Ranger. He's the son of Moriko, the weaver. She makes such lovely fabrics. Maybe I should bring her to live in Queensdale."

"That would be most unusual, Majesty," he remarks, biting back what he'd really like to say, "since no Humans live there, and besides, she'd be separated from her homestead and her flock of sheep so she wouldn't do her best work there. Surely you wouldn't like that."

She gives him a sideways look. "Do you know her then? Bring me more of that hibiscus mead."

He gestures to Liana to bring her drink, and she continues, "Wasn't that the village you stayed in that time I sent you to negotiate with the Raiders?"

"Yes Benevolence, that was the village. Negotiations with the Rocky Shorelanders were long and unfruitful. They had little to offer and wanted much, which I believe is still the case."

"You were gone for so long, maybe you had a dalliance with one of the Human females." She looks at him sideways. "Never mind, it's not important. I'm sure you wouldn't stray from the Royal chambers." She continues on, nattering about unimportant things.

He listens to the irritating prattle that he must endure in order to keep the Queendom out of the hands of the duplicitous Lord Jarin and his faction of greedy courtiers. Her relentless voice scrapes at his composure, never quite making an accusation, but never leaving him alone. At least she no longer invites him to the royal bedchamber. She has long suspected there might be an offspring, but he has painstakingly hidden Moriko's identity, because the Queen would do her and Caden harm, if she knew.

Liana keeps her eyes averted as she clears away the last of the refreshments. The handmaidens and Guards pretend they hear nothing.

CHAPTER 13

It sounds like a storm, but why are so many animals running? Smoke seeps under the door, and I realize it's a fire. I go to look out the door, but Gundega stops me.

"Don't. You'll just bring smoke into the cottage." She tells me to grab the cheese and nuts from a cupboard, and take half of the travel cakes from the carrysack by the door. She hobbles over with her walking stick and tucks the other half into the hood of her cape. She hands me the carrysack and one of the water skins.

She takes a deep breath and traces a complex spiraling pattern over her chest. "Strengthening Enchantment. I used it to carry you. Won't last forever, but enough to get us out of here." She adds her own water skin to her hood and then hastens us out the door into the smoky forest, hobbling quickly down the path.

The animals are racing pell-mell down the hill, and so are we, though we're going more at an angle. The smaller animals are ignored by their predators, a bear lumbers past us, a cougar with her young and a pair of deer, all running for their lives. We skirt the main trails because they're the most crowded with animals. Gundega leads the way, her stick marking time as we hasten down the mountainous path. I scurry to follow, my steps hopping down the unfamiliar path.

The smoky air rasps my nostrils, but once in a while it dissipates and the walking clears my head, blowing out more of the stink and stagnation of that awful sleeping powder. Images washed clean drift up and swirl, each step away from the cottage releasing more traces of memory. *First softly, then growing, I hear the rhythm of drums, the playful harmonies of flutes. Colorful wisps swirl in the air, dancers glowing and twirling. There's a small girl laughing at the edge of the clearing. More dancers, bright eyes sparkling at mine as they spin, the lights swirling, filling the air, turning faster and faster.* Until it's a whirlwind. Suddenly confused and panicked, I stagger. I'm panting, can't catch my breath.

Gundega stops and turns to me, "Breathe," she says as gently as her croaky voice can. "You're letting it come too fast. Slow your breathing, slow the pictures. Don't let them spin wild." She turns and keeps walking. She doesn't slow down.

I take a couple of slow breaths and do my best to keep up with her. We're not slowing down, but when the pictures come back, I can see them more clearly. *The little girl is running toward me. "Sislie, wait for me," she calls. I slow down and we grab each other's hands, spinning and laughing.*

I stumble again. Sislie? is that my name? I whisper it, not sure. The little girl's name seems to be... Carrie? Cathie? Sister? Cousin? I keep walking, now matching Gundega's stride. I breathe. I'm still scared and confused, but the panic has subsided. I concentrate on each step, maneuvering around the tree roots and occasional mounds of animal scat. The images keep coming, but slowly now.

Adult faces. I know those faces with their wide brows over violet eyes. Fae faces. I am Fae. Right. That's why I recognized that Lynx sigil on Gundega's shoulder. I must have a sigil too. I touch my shoulder, and a soothing hum suffuses my chest. It feels like... like home. Like I have a home. I am Fae. I am Sislie. I say it out loud, "Sislie."

"What?"

"Sislie. I. Am. Sislie."

"Yes, you are, and you'd better keep up if we're going to make it to the cave. Those Raiders started the fire, but they don't travel by night, and they didn't see us, so we should be safe there."

I am Sislie. My heart grows, and I feel something I haven't had for a long time. I'm glad! I do a little pirouette and almost trip into a bramble bush next to the path. As I scamper to catch up, a new set of images fills my mind. *A dozen glowing Fae weave and twirl in the middle of a clearing, their wings unfurled, silken, gossamer, shimmering as they gracefully swirl and drape down the backs of the dancers—who flicker in and out of view.* I know this! I think I can do this! I feel a tingling in my back, in my shoulder blades. I feel a glow.

"Stop that!" Gundega turns, an angry scowl on her face. "You'll get us killed. That's like a beacon to the Queen's Guards. They are surely looking for us, and they can sense it from far away."

I wilt, confused again, tears springing to my eyes. Glow faded, tingling gone. Dancing gone. Lips trembling, I carry on, trying not to stumble. I'm stuck with her and I hate her.

We trudge for ages in the choking smoke, not stopping for anything. Finally, we come to a steep rock face with scrubby bushes growing at its base. The path runs parallel to it for a while, then veers off. But Gundega heads straight into the bush. She uses her stick to part it from its neighbors and reveals a burlap flap. It's the opening of a cave. I stoop through the low entrance.

The cave is big, much bigger than her cottage, even though its opening is small. The walls are smooth rock for the most part, and there's a faint light coming from a crack in the ceiling. Thankfully, no smoke has gotten in. It has a faint, earthy smell and no trace of having been used by animals. The floor is sparsely strewn with twigs and stones.

"Is this your cave?" I ask.

She finishes inspecting the floor and walls of the cave. "Yes. I stayed here long ago while I was watching the cottage to make sure nobody would claim it." She begins to dismantling a tumble of rock and debris at one edge, revealing a hidden stash of firewood and a couple of rough blankets. "Take this," she says, handing one of them to me. "You'll need it tonight. It's not safe to light a fire with Raiders so close, they could see the smoke going up through the vent."

She unpacks her hood and points to my carrysack. "I always keep emergency supplies in case I need to leave in a hurry."

I'm tired, still droopy from the harsh scolding she gave me on the path. I feel sullen and resentful, angry, frustrated, scared.

Feelings. And questions, still churning in my brain. I want to know who I am, what I am. I want to know why she held me captive. And what's that shouting in my dreams about? And dancing? Was that what I'm supposed to do? Was there something about a cousin? Why were they crying? The flow of images has stopped, replaced by an uneasy emptiness in my gut.

She motions me to sit and be quiet. She draws a swirling pattern in the air facing the door of the cave. She repeats it, reaching upward toward the vent, scrawny arm sticking out of her rough-hewn sleeve. Then again, over my head and over her own. By the third time, I recognize this enchantment. I get a momentary image of a different arm extending gracefully from an embroidered sleeve, its hand tracing the same pattern, teaching it to me. It's the Unnoticeable ward, to keep others from paying attention to us. Right. I'm Fae. I know these things.

She hands me a candle and flint from her sack, and pulls out some cheese and travel cakes, which we share. We each have our own water skin. Now I understand why she always insisted they stay full by the door of the cottage.

"The Raiders are stupid and lazy, so they start scrub fires to chase the game toward their hunters. These ones did a poor job. The fire will eventually burn out. But it'll take a while."

She gathers the blanket under her and reclines on one elbow, gingerly shielding her wounded leg. I kneel at her side. I'm a healer. I'm still bitter towards her, but deeper than that, I feel my duty to heal. I cup my hands around the swollen knee. "Who are the Queen's Guards?" I ask.

She closes her eyes and sinks down on the blanket, mumbling, "Talk later. Too tired."

It's been an exhausting day, and by the time I'm finished with the healing, I'm almost asleep too. The old blanket is scratchy but warm, and I wrap it around myself and fall into a deep sleep.

I wake to the sound of tiny bells—or am I dreaming? *A dozen Fae dance at a festival. The music of flutes soars above me, and light, intricate drumming rhythms feel like fingers playing all over my body. The dancers glow as they flicker in and out of sight. Tiny gold and silver lights drift through the clearing, and when the dancers twirl, the lights create a little whirlwind around them.*

The music suffuses my body and opens my senses wide and deep. I reach out and feel the forest beyond the smoke and fire. I feel the furry warmth of rabbits and mice nestling against one another, tucked safely in their burrows. I taste the freshness of a stream and smell the sweet berries nearby. I see the Raiders, roughly encamped, the carcass of a deer hanging from a tree, blood still draining into a leather pail hanging beneath its throat. I feel the stones. They are still. I recognize the familiar thread of life flowing through all of these, causing their hearts to beat, nourishing and refreshing, and repairing small wounds and sickness as they sleep.

Gundega is asleep near me, muttering. My healing sense reaches out to the still angry knee, cooling and soothing the swelling, repairing the torn ligaments.

She awakes and looks at me with soft eyes. The cave is filled with a golden-violet light, and I am dancing. I feel like I'm floating in the air. I see her, and know her, her pain, her loss, the loneliness, a bit of madness, her tragically broken wing nubs that will never grow, never glow. Tears spill from my eyes and I contemplate what she might have been. She'll never be truly Fae again, doomed to premature aging from the magic of her shriveled wing nubs sapping her life force as it keeps trying to fulfil its fruitless task, to develop her wings, her lost heritage.

"Don't pity me," she whispers. "I am what I am. There's no going back to change it."

I know it too, and as I glow, my heart softens towards her with something like affection.

Also I know myself, who I am. I have the heartfire that makes me a healer. I can feel the flow of life through someone's body, and cleanse what's contaminated, straighten what's crooked, coax what's growing wrong to right itself. I sense all living things. And I am a dancer. It's the joy of my life, to be a dancer of the Hummingbird Clan.

And I know that little girl. She's my little cousin, Cathrie. And my mother and father. I have a home, a family, a Clan, and a destiny.

A destiny. Oh no. A groan escapes me and my gut clenches. My cousin Marielle. Marielle, who was clever and wise. Marielle, who was to be the new Queen of the Fae. Marielle, who was murdered on her way to Queensdale to train for the Grand Conclave, where the Clans gather to anoint their new Queen. Marielle, who I'm supposed to replace.

Now the shouting dreams make sense. It was me, shouting with my parents and the other Clan elders. Shouting and refusing. I'm a dancer. I don't want to be Queen. I never wanted to be Queen. I'm not fit to be Queen of the Fae. Marielle was the one who's levelheaded, smart and learned, who studied history and diplomacy. And governance. And liked it. There's no way you can force me to be Queen Designate.

Except there is. It's for the good of the Clan. For the good of the Queendom. I'm now the only female of our Clan who can fulfil our duty to provide the next Queen, in the convoluted succession that rotates among the three High Fae Clans. The death of a Queen designate has never happened before, so I always assumed being next in line was just symbolic. But not now. I'm the only one of the Hummingbird Clan who's a trained healer, fully fledged, and young enough. I'm supposed to do something that heals the land, but I don't remember what that is. It's for the good of all who inhabit our beautiful land. For the good of everyone, except me. I'm to set aside my dancing. To relinquish what gives my life beauty, grace and joy.

The jarring memory assaults me. The day before my departure for Queensdale, I slipped out for one last dance in my glade. For one last leap, twirl and *flicker*. For a last moment of freedom before I become servant of all the Fae, servant of the land. For a last moment of bliss until I was thrust into an orange sack and carried away to the hidden cottage by this strange old woman, who's not really old, and not really a woman at all.

I have a destiny. And I hate it.

CHAPTER 14

Back in the village, he tries to look for his Baba, to ask her for some salve for his burns. He wants to tell her about the birds, but his Da beats him for disappearing all day where there's work to be done. Fortunately, the back of his hand misses the blistered skin, which is mostly on his belly and forearms. Minason prepares their meal, hungrily gulping mouthfuls of rabbit stew while it's cooking. There won't be any left once Da gets hold of it.

Afterwards, he goes to find Baba, but she's not at her hut. He looks for the salve on her one shelf, which holds a couple of bowls and small clay pots above a small table. The smallest one contains the salve she's given him in the past, and he dips his finger in, to smear on his scorched belly and arms.

That night he can't sleep, and he sneaks out before dawn to visit his birds. They're trying to scramble over the branches at the entrance to the cave, wings still dragging on the ground. He hastily grabs more boughs and fashions a sturdier barrier across the cave mouth. Is he imagining things, or are they already bigger since yesterday? The birds are hissing and snorting, futilely searching the cave for prey. He hurries to find more food for them. This time he visits three different mouse nests. He hovers, motionless as a cat, waiting for each tiny animal to appear at the mouse hole, then scoops it up with his quick hands. He feeds the birds three mice each, then they flop down on the ground and fall asleep.

The days tumble by. Amazement and exhaustion rule his life in turns as he races up and down the mountain, dodging his father's slaps and punches in the village, and frantically hunting for the increasingly ravenous birds at the top. Sometimes he can only get away at night. He snatches bits of sleep between feedings. He has to find bigger prey as the birds grow. Mice are replaced by gophers, then rabbits that he now only stuns before serving, because the birds prefer their meals alive.

They're now bigger than the falcons that populate the mountain, their scales glowing dully in the cave. Their eyes have taken on a shining intensity, swirling when they look at him. Their impossibly long wings are gaining strength, and they can now tuck them to their sides instead of dragging them on the ground. Their limbs evince a sturdy muscularity that he knows will soon defeat whatever barrier he raises at the mouth of their cave.

Minason treasures his secret. He has drawn the not-so-scrawny birds on a small pottery shard with the burnt end of a stick. He carries it with him, hanging from a cord tucked inside his shirt. He's been too busy tending his birds to look for his Baba, but one morning she comes across him sitting on a rock and gazing at the picture.

"What're you doing with that picture of baby dragons?"

"Baby dragons?" He splutters and leaps to his feet, tucking the treasure back into his shirt. "What's that, Baba?"

The stern look on her face softens as she squints up at her tall grandson. Her chin slightly forward, the creases from her crooked smile accentuate a single raised eyebrow. "Long ago there were dragons, or maybe it's just a story. Come, I'll show you."

Short and bent over, with a thin body and knobbly elbows, she leads him on a circuitous route around the outer edge of the Asmung village, to a tumble-down remnant of wall from ancient times, hidden behind the women's lodge.

Minason has seen bricks and tiles like these at the midden. They provide some of his drawing materials. The old woman pushes aside some bushes to reveal crumbling stairs going down into what looks like a cave. He cautiously follows her down. The passage opens to what was once a grand hall, bigger than anything in the village, bigger than any structure he's ever seen. Most of the roof has collapsed, leaving it open to the sky. Two of the walls are caved in piles of rubble, but the third wall—Minason has no words for what he sees. It's a wall of wonders. Not just drawings, it's a giant colorful mosaic of nature, and giants, battling one another. And birds. Oh gods! Enormous colored birds with scales, with unimaginable wing spans. A grand hall Birds with fire shooting out of their mouths.

"These are the dragons," the old woman says, smiling at his gaping mouth, "and here are the babies." She points to the other standing wall, depicting a clutch of large eggs at the opening of a cave. Some are silver and turquoise streaked like his were, and others are different colors. All are shiny. A few are broken open, scrawny birds flopping on the ground nearby.

"So, where did you get that picture?" Her steely look cowers him, even though he didn't do anything wrong. "Did you steal it from here?"

"No Baba, I've never seen this place before. What is it?"

"This old ruin is from the time before remembering. We hid the entrance, and it became the women's secret place, where we can remember the old ways, and where we can hide from the men when they are angry. Back when my own grandmother was a child, women were respected elders. We made useful crafts and traded with other villages and towns, sometimes even with the Fae."

"The Fae? You mean those are real? The kids I grew up with call me fairy. Why?"

She sits down on a large stone bench and pats the seat beside her, inviting him to join her. "Your Da never wanted you to know this, but I should have told you. Your mother was Fae. Her name was Mina. That's where Minason, your name, comes from."

"Minason. Son of Mina. My mother was a Fae? She lived here?"

"She was kidnapped for the tribe because your Uncle Brom thought the Fae could cure us. He couldn't make her produce a child for him, so he gave her to your Da. She died giving birth to you. You are the only half-Fae ever born to us. That's why you're different. That's why you are quick, and tall. That's why you love beauty and look for it with those violet eyes of yours.

"The water here is poisoned. The whole mountain is poisoned. And the tribe is poisoned. That's why the men have become angry bullies, and the women have lost their power. Long ago, Fae healers came to tell us about the poison and advised us to leave this place and live elsewhere. There are safe valleys and slopes not too far from here. But by then it was too late. The men called them liars and accused the Fae of wanting to steal their hunting grounds.

"So the Fae never returned. Except for one ancient female, Ylva, who sometimes appears in the women's hut to bring us healing herbs and tell us stories of the past, including the time before remembering. She's the one who told us about the dragons. She teaches us to remember kindness, how to help women in childbirth, and other healing. The grandmothers have vowed to remember the stories, but the tribe is dwindling and there are few grandmothers left.

"But you, Minason, it doesn't seem to have affected you as much as the rest of us. You could go and live in First Bend, the Human town, and make a decent life for yourself."

"No, I couldn't leave you, or my birds."

"What birds?" She looks at him sternly again.

"I… I didn't find the drawing, Baba. I made it. My drawings, the rocks, the eggs, the big crack, the steam vent…." He stammers, he's panting, he gasps. The words tumble out of his mouth, "The stones, cave broke, so hot, the eggs, shiny streaks, the birds."

"Minason," she places her knobbly hands on his shoulders, "Look at me. Breathe. Breathe again. Look at me. Breathe slowly."

It's hard for him to look directly at his Baba, he's so used to averting his gaze so he won't be noticed. But his gasping subsides and his pounding heart slows as he looks into his Baba's eyes, steadied by the only kind hands he's ever known. "The earthshake broke my cave at the top of the mountain and opened a big crack. It was hot and smoky and red at the bottom, and my shiny rocks turned into eggs. They cracked open and the scrawny birds, um, baby dragons, came out. There are two. And they are hungry, so hungry all the time."

"Take me there."

"Baba, it's hard to get up there. I don't want you to get hurt." He takes her bony hands in his and looks earnestly into her eyes. "The paths are steep and there's a really big gap to get over."

"Don't be foolish, child. I'm as strong as you are, even if I'm old." She adjusts the bandanna wrapped around her thin hair and firms her gaze. "Let's get going." She picks up two water skins from under some rags beside a pile of rubble. "We keep a few things here in case one of the women needs to hide for a while. Here, take one." She hands it to him, along with a dry biscuit made of the taro roots that grow by the river. Minason doesn't like them because they have an acrid taste, and he has always tried to eat other things. But he accepts one from his Baba and tucks it in his pocket.

They steal away from the village up a seldom used path behind the ruin. Minason leads his Baba up the narrow trail. He holds her hand, careful not to let her slip on the loose rubble left behind after the earth shake. She keeps insisting that he doesn't need to do that, but her thankful smile when he helps her over a fallen log says something different.

When they get to the crevasse, he adds another small log to his bridge. He edges across sideways, taking both her hands in his, saying "Careful, careful, careful...."

The old woman never flinches and never looks down, but grips his hand and feels for each step before she puts her weight on it. When they're most of the way across, her foot slips on the mossy log. "Baba!" he screams. He barely manages to brace himself on the logs and keep her from pitching into the steep gully. Heart pounding, he guides her the rest of the way across.

When they reach the other side, she is panting and shaking. "I need to sit down for a minute." She sits on a fallen log across their path and takes a sip of water from her skin. "I'll be ok."

He sits beside her on the log as they both catch their breath. Then, "Baba, tell me more about the dragons."

"I never saw them myself, because they were long gone. But that ancient Fae told a story of dragons breathing fire, long ago, when Dragon's End Mountain was a volcano. They fed off a kind of chunky lava, called a-a, while it was still red and burning. You've never seen it, and never will. But those prickly black rocks near our village were once that kind of lava. It didn't flow smoothly from the volcano, but crunched slowly out of the hot fissures in the mountain. The dragons chewed it and that's how they got their fiery breath. So, if your birds are really dragons, they'll never have fire. Because the mountain doesn't spew fire any more, just bits of steam here and there."

"But Baba, yes it does. The earth shake split my cave and turned it into a wide crack. It's big and there's hot red down there. It's really hot, and I burned my belly trying to save the eggs," he said, lifting his shirt to show the partially healed scorch marks across his belly and chest.

"Then let's get going," she pushes herself up and climbs over the log she was resting on.

Minason clambers after her, then takes the lead, still holding her hand to steady her. He's eager to see his birds—his dragons—again. Now almost the size of wolves, their gawkishness has transformed into a robust muscularity and their turquoise scales have taken on a dull but steady glow. He knows they'll be hungry, and wants to hurry, but he keeps his pace slow so his Baba can keep up.

When they get to the top, the barrier to the cave is demolished. The dragons are finishing off the remains of a luckless racoon that skulked across their clearing at the wrong time. They gobble the bloody carcass with much hissing and snorting, then look around for more food, their sharp fangs dripping crimson. They spot Minason and Baba, golden eyes scrutinizing the newcomer.

Baba's eyes widen in fear, and she's rooted to the spot. She doesn't hear him scream "Run, Baba!" as he realizes the dragons might look on her as prey. The birds waddle toward them, long sharp talons clicking on the rock surface, golden eyes swirling.

He grabs her hand and tries to pull her to safety, but she's enchanted by their gaze, and unable to move. Their waddling gait is surprisingly fast as they approach, wings neatly tucked at their sides. He starts to shout and jump and wave his arms, trying to chase them away. He frantically looks for a stick to hit them with.

But his shouts turn to relieved laughter as the no longer scrawny birds rub against him with their snouts and foreheads. They're just nuzzling and he happily scratches them under the chin, where the scales are soft, one of the few places where they welcome a caress. Content that their Minason has returned, they turn to his Baba, sniff her all over, then raise their chins for another scratch. She cautiously raises her hand to comply and they snort and hiss. It sounds to him like purring.

"See Baba? They're friendly, just like kittens."

The young dragons lumber back to the clearing and spread their wings, flapping them and hopping around, trying vainly to fly. Her laugh as she watches them is just a bit nervous.

CHAPTER 15

"Stupid girl." She hurls the headpiece across the room, her handmaidens aghast as the jewelled treasure lands with a thump on the silk carpet. Her piercing scowl is as sharp as her words. "It's too tight on my forehead and you're always pulling my hair with those metal pins. You know I like the coral ones."

"I'm so sorry majesty, the coral ones got broken." Liana doesn't mention that her Majesty broke the last precious emerald tipped coral pin last time she had a tantrum.

"Clumsy nitwit, you broke them and now I have to make do with the metal ones. You know they pull and they are so drab." Her voice scrapes the ear and the nerves, each barbed word repudiating the elegance of the sumptuous dressing room. "Never mind that," she stops Liana from picking up the headpiece. "Fetch Ned."

"But Splendid One," Liana drops to a curtsy, "they await you. Lord Kairon is ready to escort you to the throne room."

"I didn't give you permission to speak." Her chin drops, and Queen Maelys, exhausted by her own tirade, closes her eyes for a moment.

... Stupid, stupid, clumsy girl... so young.. so stupid.... She drifts into reverie, forgetting Liana, forgetting Ned, forgetting the delegation, forgetting the headpiece, remembering being young, being beautiful, being adored.

Twirling in his arms under sparkling lights at the Moon Festival ball, all the High Fae applauding as they dance. Such a beautiful couple, elegant and brilliant. He could always entice a smile when she was having a vexatious day. He was her beloved, admired by everyone.

But when whispers of betrayal crept around the palace like thieves, they robbed her of her trust and, finally, her Guard had to cause the terrible accident. How she cried for an entire season after they found his shattered body at the bottom of the cliff, wings tattered, body broken beyond the skill of any healer. And then of course the assassin had to disappear, so no one would ever know. Faithful Jarin arranged it all. It was so tragic, her heart broken, slowly turning to stone.

She drifts deeper, her thin mouth going slack as a drop of drool appears on her chin. She sighs and mutters.

Liana doesn't catch what she says. "Precious Majesty, Splendid Queen, they await you." She tentatively pats the royal shoulder.

She startles awake, still in bliss until she notices the jewelled and feathered headpiece on the floor. "Come here," she scolds the stoic handmaiden and slaps her face. "Imbecile! You've dropped my headpiece again. Don't you realize it's worth more than your whole Clan? I should send you back to your village."

Liana falls on her knees. "Sorry, sorry, your Magnificence, I'm too clumsy." She scuttles over to the headpiece, relieved to find it undamaged. The last time the Queen had beaten her, her wing nubs were sore for weeks and her Majesty forbade her from visiting the healers. She sighs and pins the elaborate headpiece back on the royal head, silently enduring the barrage of complaints and criticism. She fetches the Queen's favorite jewelled slippers and gestures to the other handmaiden to pick up the royal jewelled salamander in its gilded cage.

"Is Kairon here?"

"Yes, Splendid Majesty, he's been in your morning room this last hour."

"Tell him to get in here. I'm tired of always having to wait for him."

Liana scurries to open the door where the Royal Consort waits, impassive, for his Queen. He enters the dressing room, bows, and offers his arm, "Gracious Eminence, they await your pleasure."

Liana and the other handmaidens curtsy. She avoids looking at Kairon as he escorts the queen through the ornately carved door. Nobody notices the small folded paper he slips into her hand as he passes her. She opens the note and quickly scans it, then closes the door and follows the entourage to her throne room.

Their entrance into the throne room triggers a wave of lustrous silk, velvet, and glittering jewels as the courtiers and ladies bow to greet their Queen. The hall has curved walls, as do most of the rooms of the royal palace, formed of trees coaxed and enticed, often for many years, by the most skilled artisans of the coaxer Clans—grown together and molded into the halls, dining and drawing rooms, gaming rooms, bedrooms, and bathing chambers of the palace.

Clusters of will-o'-the-wisps form chandeliers, and sumptuous colorful tapestries adorn the walls. Kairon helps her step up onto the dais where her Lord Chamberlain Jarin awaits her arrival. He is a Fae of indeterminate age, pale, icy violet eyes set high in his forehead, accentuated by his straight eyebrows and bald head. Unlike the other Fae at court, he displays a trim white beard and moustache. He greets the Queen with a brief but formal bow, which nevertheless signals that he has been waiting patiently.

She leans on Kairon's arm until she is seated and then impatiently pushes it aside. She looks critically around the room and points to one of her courtiers. "Damon, straighten your cravat and don't make me see such slovenly appearance again." She's oblivious of how the courtiers and ladies cringe at her shrill and jangling voice.

She gestures to the herald. "I will see this so-called delegation."

There's a brief scuffle at the door as the herald announces a delegation from the Rocky Shores. The Queen's Guard drag in five Raiders and fling them to the floor at the foot of her throne. Four of them are badly beaten.

One Raider, a tall broad-shouldered man with bright black eyes and a bald head, rises to his knees. He is uninjured, evidently the leader of the delegation. His clothing is finer than the others, and he wears a golden earring and several gold chains around his neck. In a commanding voice he announces, "Majesty, and all the Clans, we of the Rocky Shores come to offer our abject and humble apology and reparation for the death of your young apprentice, Marielle."

On hearing this, the Queen's Guard and most of the courtiers draw their swords and surge forward, but the Queen raises her hand to stay them. She addresses the Raider. "What is your name, Raider?"

"Chance of the Rocky Shores, Your Majesty," he proclaims, attempting a formal style of speech.

She knows who they are but asks anyway, "and who are you of the Rocky Shores?"

"We are the children and grandchildren of sailors, merchants and pirates shipwrecked on the north end of your glorious land, Eminence, beyond the peninsula. Our settlement has grown larger than the rugged coast can support. We're not Raiders, though alas, a few from our settlement have ventured into such activities. We work to establish the rule of law," he gestures to the battered miscreants on the floor, "but these four have opposed us."

He notices the Queen about to say something, but talks louder and faster, his confident voice taking on a petulant tone. "If we Shorelanders had better land, none of this would have happened. We have sent many delegations to you, hoping to establish trade and relations with the other Humans of the Land, and with the Fae. These were always refused, until now."

"And now?" A hard glitter comes to the Queen's eyes. Her voice is ice.

He tries to get up on his feet but one of the Guards knocks him down. Again, he gets up on his knees. "And now, Majesty, we have unwittingly been involved in the most horrific of crimes." He gestures to the four sprawled on the floor, "These four ruffians took it on themselves to try to kidnap Marielle, the young Queen in waiting. They meant to hold her for ransom, but her Honor Guard fought fiercely, and in the melee that followed, an errant crossbow bolt found the young Queen-to-be."

"My Queen's Guard are unsurpassed warriors. How were they so easily killed?"

"The ruffians stole crossbows from our armory. We think the Guards sensed their presence, but didn't know about the crossbows, so they didn't recognize the Raiders as a threat. Several of your warriors were dead before they even knew there was an attack." Again, he tries to get up, and is knocked down by the Guards. "We have already punished these ones, but we bring them to you, to do with as you will. And in reparation, we bring you these two chests of treasures, the last of what we salvaged from our ships. There are rare jewels and precious glass containers and ornaments not made in your land. And gold and silver bullion."

"What are these crossbows? Show them to me."

"Humblest apology, Majesty, I didn't bring a weapon with me. They're a short bow that launches its arrow with a winding mechanism. It doesn't require the same skill as a longbow, which most of our people don't have the training for."

"We accept your reparation, and will take your prisoners to meet their just fate. We will let you go. But know this. Killers of Fae can never be forgiven. There will be no trade between us. You will never be welcome in our Land." She gestures to the Guards, who drag away the wounded ruffians. "You will be escorted to the peninsula. Tell your people if any of your ilk is seen on our side of the peninsula, they'll be executed immediately. And now we know about the crossbows." She turns to her Lord Chamberlain, "Jarin, see to the decree."

This time, the Guards don't stop Chance from rising to his feet. "Majesty, you will regret this." His dark scowl annuls the genteel demeanor he has tried to exhibit until now. "Our numbers grow, and there's not enough arable land on the Rocky..."

Her pointed finger stops his words as the Guards shove him out of the throne room, "Get him out of my sight."

CHAPTER 16

"We have to stay here until the Raiders move on." Gundega takes out two of the travel cakes and sits down on her makeshift sleeping pallet. She beckons me and hands me one. "Sit, I'll tell you the rest."

After an exhausted sleep, I'm feeling restless. Anxious about the fire that's still raging outside the cave. Frustrated. Angry with her for kidnapping me, angry with myself for letting her trick me. Still confused about what's going on. But here I am trapped with my captor, who refuses to explain why she kidnapped me. There's nothing I can do about it right now, so I call on my dancer's self-discipline and settle down cross-legged on the blanket to listen.

"Finding the cabbage and that pot was my first hint that there could be safety, that I might have a home. When I first saw it, the cottage was in shambles. I watched it for a whole year to make sure it wasn't a travelers' shelter, and had been truly abandoned. I slept in trees for the rest of the summer, and when the weather got cold, I moved to this cave. There were plenty of dried leaves and grasses for a sleeping pallet and for the first I could remember I had the comfort of a soft bed. I ate berries and nuts and roots, harvested the rest of the cabbage, and hunted small game.

"There's a Fae village nearby, home of the Squirrel Clan, partly in the trees. I never tried to go in or talk to them, never thought I'd be safe there or welcome."

"But Gundega, you were a young Fae. They would have taken you in and helped you."

"I didn't know that. I couldn't trust anyone, and I was so young when they took me. I didn't really even know I was Fae. I just watched the children playing at the edge of the village and listened to their talk. I watched them for years, yearning to be like them but sure I could never enter their world. Often their play was practicing small glamours and enchantments. I worked the spells on my own, copied them exactly. The pose, the hand gesture, the look on their face. But it never worked. I almost gave up, but then I discovered there was a kind of *intention* that would fuel the spell. It wasn't just the words or hand movements.

"I learned one for hunting small animals. First, I glamoured a rabbit to come to me, thinking it would make a fine stew. But it felt wrong to kill it and eat it, so I let it go. I could eat rabbit, but only if I caught it the usual way with a snare or a sling."

She notices me stirring uneasily and looks at me with her lop-sided grin, "Don't worry, there was never meat in the stews I gave you. I could tell by your smell that you don't eat animal flesh."

Gundega shifts around and leans toward me. Her voice is becoming more accustomed to talking, and losing some of the croakiness as the story pours from her memory. "My biggest accomplishment was the Unnoticeable ward. Once I mastered this, I glamoured the hut so the eyes of passers-by would slide off it. Then I fixed it up with tools I stole in the Human village down in the valley. The Unnoticeable spell was very useful there too, because I could sneak around mostly unseen, and people would think they had just misplaced the things I took. I didn't do it very often, or from the same villager more than once, so they wouldn't suspect there was something going on. Once I almost got caught stealing a pie cooling on a porch, but I ran fast. I didn't even mind the stomach ache I got from gobbling it down all at once. I stole tools, rope, blankets, utensils, clothing, shoes. I did the same with vegetables, seeds, and a rug.

"Another glamour I learned was the Magnification spell, how to appear very large. One time I stared down a bear with that one. I was never afraid of anything after that.

"The Fae never paid attention to me. I always kept a distance from the children I was watching, never talked to them or let them see me. I thought the Fae either hadn't noticed me—which was unlikely, since the Fae notice everything—or weren't interested in me. I hoped not."

"But one day, two Fae Warriors came to my garden and ordered me to come with them. They escorted me down the mountain path, one in front and one behind. As we walked, I tried to figure out what they wanted. But their speech was so fast that I couldn't understand most of what they were saying. I picked up a few words, 'spy, crazy, weird.' They wouldn't answer my questions. They stopped in a small glade and one of the Warriors traced a complicated enchantment in the air. He spoke words that buzzed in my ears like swarming bees, and some kind of opening appeared in front of us. They pushed me through it and we were in another glade. They did this a few more times, and in this way we travelled all the way down the mountain in less than a day."

Gundega is lost in the memory. Anger and frustration forgotten, I'm riveted by her story.

They travel down the mountain to the central valley between the mountains. The last portal leads them to an astonishing town at the far end. Queensdale Palace, they deign to tell her. Grand structures are made of trees grown into shapes that hold rooms inside. Stairways spiral up into the trees and vines dripping with white and violet blossoms decorate all the buildings, wafting their sweet fragrance. Gardens burst with rainbows of color and small trees bear a large yellow fruit she has never seen.

Even though amazed at her surroundings, she tries to escape when she realizes they're bringing her to the most fantastic of these buildings. But one of the Guards traces two small circles in the air beside her. It's like the enchantment she once learned for small animals, and she stops struggling. She meekly walks beside them.

The entrance is enormous, palatial. She can't see the whole thing from where they take her. Hallways spiral off in all directions. They lead her down one of these, passing splendid glowing rooms decorated with multicolored tapestries. They're walking too fast for her to get more than a glimpse into any of them. Eventually they enter a luxurious chamber full of exquisite furnishings grown into the shapes of chairs, settees, and tables. The walls are draped with luminous tapestries.

An ancient, sharp featured Fae sits on an ornately carved chair resting on a dais at the far end of the room. She wears a silken, pearl embroidered gown and a headdress with long blue and red feathers rising from its forehead. And a Youthfulness glamour. An old courtier with pale violet eyes in a long face stands beside her.

The warriors throw Gundega on the ground before the dais. When she tries to get up, they knock her down, and one of them nudges her with his foot. "Kneel before Her Majesty." She tries to use her Magnification glamour but they flick it aside like a gnat. She sits on the floor and looks up at the old Majesty.

The Queen of the Fae scowls down at her with small, purple eyes. She waves the Guards and courtier away. She says something, her thin lips barely moving. Her voice has a shrill buzz that bores into Gundega's ears, her speech so rapid that she can only take in a few words. When she stares at her blankly, the old Fae raises a jewel-encrusted hand and draws a complicated pattern in the air between them, then speaks again.

Gundega stares away toward the entrance of the cave as she remembers the conversation.

"What are you, and why do you spy on my young?" Now she can understand every word clearly.

"Gundega. I like to watch them." She feels a compulsion to reply, but her voice croaks, unaccustomed to speaking.

"Show me your shoulder."

Again, a compulsion to obey. She draws her shift down over her shoulder.

"This is a broken sigil of the Lynx Clan. How did this come to be?"

"I don't know, maybe it broke while I was running from the Asmung."

"The crazy ones. I suppose they wanted you for their misguided attempts to breed."

"I think so, my friend Mina—she died having their child."

"So you ran all the way to Cougar Mountain. You must have come into fledging time while you were running. You were sick or starving, so your wings never developed. Look at you. You look like an old Human."

A tiny wisp of hope flutters out of her mouth, almost unbeknownst to her. "Could I go back to my clan?"

The Queen's eyes are as cold as her voice. "No. They wouldn't want you now, broken and disfigured as you are. You'd be an embarrassment, a pathetic cripple, with your puny spells, looking like an old Human. If they took you in out of pity, they might let you live at the outskirts of the village, and put you to cleaning the latrines."

Whatever hope was left to her dies. She will never have a family or a clan or any home other than her solitary cottage.

My chest aches as I feel the flood of anguish from this wrongfully aged and broken Fae. Gundega never had a chance. She'll never be Fae, never cast any but the simplest of spells that many Humans can do. I shudder to imagine what it would be like to lose my wings, my abilities. She stops talking and looks away to the far corner of the cave. We sit in silence.

After a few minutes, she stretches out her injured knee and takes a couple of sips from her waterskin. "She made me promise to spy on the Squirrel Clan, and also the Human villagers. She particularly wanted me to keep my eye out for a young half-Fae from First Bend. Afterward, the Guards escorted me to the outskirts of Queensdale. By then it was dark, but they left me to find my own way back up the mountain. I still felt the compulsion to do her bidding, but I was angry. And hungry. I hadn't had anything to eat since early morning when they came to get me.

"As I stood out there trying to figure out how to get home, another ancient Fae approached and invited me to follow her. This one didn't wear the Youthfulness glamour, and her wings draped softly from her shoulders instead of being tucked away. Her voice and manner were soft, and I felt reassured in her presence. She said her name was Ylva, and told me she was the oldest of the Fae.

"She led me to her chalet at the edge of Queensdale. She gave me food and drink, and a better cloak and shoes than what I had on. She cleansed me of the Queen's enchantments, and gave me a Protection spell that would let me brush off any glamours cast on me without my permission. She gave me a soft bed to sleep that night. In the morning, she sent one of her attendants to escort me back to my cottage, through several portals, but different ones than the Queen's Guards had used.

"After a few months, Queen Maelys sent for me again, but this time she was very pleasant. She gave me fine cakes and mead, and taught me a new spell, the one you saw, which would make me really strong for a short time. I told her what little I knew. There was nothing about the young half-Fae lad, but she appeared to be satisfied with my report. She didn't see that the Compulsion glamour was gone. Anything about me was beneath her notice. She gave me some tisanes and sent me on my way. Her Guards escorted me back to the cottage this time and treated me with courtesy. Over the next few years, she sent for me several times, and I began to trust her. I didn't see Ylva again.

"But then Marielle was killed and everything changed."

CHAPTER 17

The animals have fled. So has his horse, which he sent away, hoping it would find its way back to the Rangers' compound in First Bend.

He has to get to that cottage and find Sislie.

Half staggering, half running for his life, Caden fights his way through the burnt debris and thickening smoke, gasping for breath. He knows the terrain, and his uncanny sense of direction helps him gravitate toward a deep ravine he remembers, in spite of the many detours the fire forces him to make. He hopes the conflagration will leapfrog over it, so he can hunker down there until the worst of the fire passes.

Surrounded by a wall of smoke and flame, assaulted by the avalanche of noise as trees fall and the fire howls, he almost stumbles over a small spotted cat, lost or abandoned by its mother. Without thinking, he scoops it up and tucks it into his jacket. It nestles into his chest and starts rooting for a teat. A momentary trace of amusement clears his vision, and he spots a thinning in the smoke.

He turns to dash through to the ravine, but suddenly there's a loud explosion above the din and one of the old trees begins to topple to the ground, taking with it several smaller ones. He takes off as fast as he can run. But a falling tree knocks him down and traps him under one of its branches.

Stunned, he's suddenly lying on his back, gasping. The little cat wriggles deeper into his jacket. His arm hurts, though he doesn't seem to have any other injury. It's trapped just below the elbow, under a branch about the same thickness as his muscular forearm. The branch is growing out of the trunk of a small birch. Small, but big enough to trap him. He pulls his arm, but it won't budge.

Caden doesn't panic. Near the ground, the air is not as bad and he can catch his breath. He pulls a few more times, but to no avail. He tries to wedge his legs around so he can push the tree away with his feet, but he's too close to it. He manages to wriggle his large hunting knife out from the sheath attached to his belt, then stabs the wood and curses. The branch is fresh and hard. There's no way he can saw through it.

He still doesn't panic, but restrained by the tree and his awkward position, he can't see very far to look for an implement he might use to extricate himself. He feels around for a piece of wood he could shove under the branch and possibly lever it upwards. Nothing big or strong enough, and no rock to use as a fulcrum. Next he tries to dig under the tree with his hunting knife, hoping to undermine his arm and pull it out, though even in his imperiled state he regrets the misuse of a good tool. But there are too many stones and roots and he makes no headway.

His breathing gets weaker as another blast of thick smoke billows towards him. Now he's fighting panic, realizing he is completely trapped.

He holds up his knife and looks at it. He looks at his arm. He looks at his hunting knife again. NO! There is no life for a one-armed Ranger. But then he pictures his mother, grieving, her son vanished without a trace. He takes the knife and places the tip in the center of his elbow joint. He calculates. Caden is a hunter. He knows how to cut through and dislocate a joint of meat. *Damn, damn, damn! I can do this. That's all it is. Just meat. Just do it quickly.*

He slows his breath, reaches for his carrysack that got knocked off his back. His fingers scrabble for the extra bowstring he always carries in a small pocket. He awkwardly pushes the string under his arm, and one handed, using his chin to hold the string in place and his teeth to pull the ends, ties off his arm above the elbow as a tourniquet.

Once more, he grips the knife and places the tip of the blade in the crook of his elbow. Trying to numb his fear, he musters up his fiercest resolve, aware that it's this or a horrific death, his body never to be found. A groan escapes him in anticipation of the pain and shock.

Just as he's about to plunge the knife, he opens his eyes for a moment, and imagines he can see Sislie. Her face seems to emerge from the billowing smoke. Not laughing this time, but smudged with soot and a panic-stricken look on her face. She grabs the hand gripping his knife and pulls it back from making the cut. He struggles, but weakly. "I dreamed about you." And he faints.

He wakes up, confused. The air has cleared a bit. Two women are digging around his arm. One is old, she croaks, "Dig down right there under his elbow, then we can pull him out. The young one takes a small shovel and plunges it into the earth beside his elbow, stomping on it several times for a deeper scoop. Then she climbs over his arm and does the same on the other side. After several stomps, the earth under his arm abruptly collapses, opening a big hole half under Caden and half under the tree. He plunges down, not even trying to catch the edge, and lands in a pile of loose earth and stones. He's in a cavern that must be an animal's lair. The air is musty, but there's little smoke. His arm is hurting but intact.

The young woman jumps down and lands lightly beside him. "Let me help you." She takes his injured arm between her hands. He can feel the purpling flesh cool as though a fresh breeze were blowing through it, and his pain subsides. She takes his face between her hands and studies his eyes.

"Sislie." He gasps.

CHAPTER 18

"Who are you?" I frown, sure I've never been distracted by those smoldering violet eyes before. "How do you know my name?"

He's still dazed from the fall. "I was looking for you. You were missing. I dreamed about you. You were dancing. And laughing. And glowing. And you're beautiful."

Gundega shouts down to us, "What are you two nattering about? Help me down. We have to get out of the fire." I help her down into the cavern, a small kitten tumbling in with her.

She turns to start down what looks like a tunnel, still limping even though I healed her knee as best I could. "Let's see where this goes. I've heard stories about dwarves' tunnels left behind after they disappeared. This must be one of them."

The tunnel is low, and we have to stoop to get through. We have no idea where we're going, but with my returning memory, I realize I can make us a light. I cup the palm of my hand and hold it in front of me. A small ball of light appears, enough to brighten the narrow passage. It's got to be safer than the forest fire. The walls are hard clay. We find some deeply etched runes close to where we landed. None of us can read them.

We haven't gone many steps when a loud crash right behind us makes us all jump. Dirt and sparks wash down the tunnel we just came from, pummeling the backs of our legs and littering the path before us. Tree branches now fill the cavern we had fallen into. There's no going back. The tunnel turns off to the left for about a hundred paces, then down some steps and carries on until we enter an enormous cavern.

"I have to rest." Gundega drops her staff and carrysack, plopping down on a rock near the entrance to the cavern. She's panting, and she groans and stretches her healing leg out in front of her. "I'll just be a minute. Let me catch my breath. I know we can't stay. We might not be safe here."

The young man closes his eyes, putting one hand on the wall over another set of runes. "We're safe here for now. There's no one in this part of the tunnel, not Human, or Fae either."

"Are you reading the runes?" I ask, again distracted by those violet eyes.

"No, I'm just *feeling* the space, the tunnel. I can sense what's around me. The forest animals have all escaped, those who didn't get killed. The fire is still raging above us. This tunnel seems to go a long way, but I can't tell how long or where it ends." He gazes at me, taking a step toward me.

I stare at him, ignoring the look in his eyes. The narrow jaw, high forehead, violet eyes just like mine. But there's something about him that's different. Yes! Human. "You're half Human, aren't you?"

"I've only ever been called half-Fae," he says, raising his eyebrows. "But yeah, that's right. My mother is Human and my father is Fae. My name is Caden. I'm a Ranger from the town of

First Bend. I was told you had disappeared, and the Hummingbird Clan is looking for you."

"Caden," Gundega squeezes her words out between fits of coughing. "I've heard that name before. But we need to keep moving."

I give her leg another healing and we take a few sips from our water skins. The little cat has followed us. It meows and rubs against Caden's foot. He cups his hands to give it some water, and it gratefully purrs and nips at his ankle. We set out and follow the only passage that leads away from the blocked entrance. He carries his bow low, at an angle, so it won't drag on the ground, because it's too long to carry upright in the sling over his shoulder.

We walk for hours. We find another cavern like the one we fell into. It appears to be the end of the tunnel, with a narrow opening leading upward, and all three of us feel an urge to follow it. When we get to the exit, it's blocked by bushes, but even without trying to push through, we can tell the fire is still raging outside and it's too hot and smoky to go out. We have to turn back. But when we get back to the cavern, it's not the end of the tunnel any more, the wall is revealed as a thinning illusion we can push through.

We walk for what seems like days. We've lost all sense of time in the dark tunnels. We come across more illusory exits like the first one, all too hot and smoky. I've been examining the runes at each entrance. They have an elven look about them, and the glyphs are the same each time. They must be connected to the urge we have to go upwards whenever the path branches that way.

We're exhausted, but we keep going. It feels like we've been walking forever. Gundega has to stop and rest more and more often. We finish the cheese and nuts from her cottage, and Caden shares the tasty travel cakes from his carrysack, which luckily fell into the tunnels with him. Finally, spent, we stumble into a cavern that has a bit of its own light. It comes from a crack in the rock at one side, also letting in a whiff of smoke. There's a large crevasse off to the side, which Caden goes to explore while I tend to Gundega's splinted leg. It's healing reasonably well, but she really needs to rest.

I help her lie down and wrap her in her cloak. She looks up at me, an indecipherable look in her eyes. "Leave me here," she whispers. "I can't go on. I'll be ok." Tears leak from her eyes when I shake my head. "I've survived worse than this. You young ones save yourselves."

"Gundega, I'm sure we can..."

Caden rushes out of the crevasse. "There's water. It's safe to drink. And some kind of diagram. It may be a map of the tunnels. But it's glamoured, and it's hard for me to examine it."

I follow him and replenish the water skins, bringing one back to Gundega, who's falling asleep. She takes a long drink and drops off.

"Let's take a look." I'm exhausted too, but curious about what he's found. It's definitely a map, glamoured with an enchantment I don't know. It feels similar to the Unnoticeable spell, making my eyes want to slide away from it. I can't remove it. It seems to be inherent in the lines etched in the rock face. But I can see through it, and trace a Revealing spell so Caden can see it too, standing close to my shoulder. Even though it's blurry to his eyes, his sense of direction is so strong that he's able to locate us about two-thirds of the way down Cougar Mountain, on the south side facing Queensdale valley.

As we peer at the map, the Revealing spell dissipates and all of a sudden my head is spinning. I reach out to lean on the wall and Caden beside me is doing the same. The cavern is whirling around us and I'm knocked off my feet, sprawling awkwardly on the ground at his feet. After a few minutes, Caden reaches down to help me up. We're both covered in a sprinkling of dust.

"We all need to rest, Sislie," he says, "I didn't realize we were this tired."

"That wasn't just tired, definitely some kind of magic, but I can't tell what it was."

"Maybe you can figure it out later. But for now, we're safe here."

I don't argue. I'm so tired I can hardly stand, and I sag against. As I fall, strong arms lift me and carry me to where Gundega is sleeping, the little cat snuggled up against her chest.

Caden cradles Sislie in his arms. Even though he's exhausted too, it's all he can do to not kiss her forehead, nuzzle her neck, rub his cheek in her curly hair. She doesn't look tired and bedraggled to him, only beautiful. Dark soot smudging her face, but beautiful. Just like in his vision when she was dancing and glowing. And she's a healer too. His injured arm hardly hurts any more, the forearm no longer throbbing, bruises fading.

Warmth suffuses his chest and a tender smile softens his lips. He places her gently next to the old woman.

The little cat comes to him as he stands and watches over the sleeping Fae and her companion. He absently picks it up and scratches under its chin, taking comfort in its purring. He carries it over to the pool and fills a small indentation in the rock with water, so it can drink. Then he sits down with the cat in his lap, feeling the space around them, wondering about the dwarves who left these tunnels behind.

They are creatures of legend, vanished long ago. He breathes slowly, to relax, and extends his senses as wide as he can. No traces of Human or Fae. Only a few small creatures taking refuge from the fire in tunnel entrances like the one they fell into. There is still a hint of smoke in the air, but the temporary safety lulls him and he leans back on the wall and sleeps.

In the morning, Gundega is the first one awake. She nudges him with her foot on her way to the pool for more water. He groans and stretches but comes fully awake as she emerges from the deepest part of the crevasse with a small sack. "Look. I found these dried out travel cakes. They're really old, but not spoiled. We can soak them in water once we run out of food. They won't taste good, but they'll keep us alive if we end up staying in the caves for a long time."

Caden's seeking sense is awake now, too. "Someone's in the tunnels, coming in our direction. They're too far for me to tell who they are, but they might be Raiders, so we should get going." They wake Sislie and hurriedly gobble some more of Caden's travel cakes before they hasten on their way.

CHAPTER 19

Caden takes up Gundega's carrysack so her load will be less. If it was only her leg, she would be ok, just slower than usual. But I'm worried about that wound on her head. There's nothing I can do about it hurrying down the tunnel, so I start asking the pent-up questions I have for Caden. I'm curious about him, but first, "How do you know my name?"

"I dreamed about you. I mean, I heard about you, too. Your Clan is desperately looking for you. They're offering a reward for finding you."

"A reward? So I'm nothing but a prize?" I had thought he was attractive, but my admiration curdles and sours. "What are you then, a hired mercenary? I thought Rangers were supposed to help people."

"We do. I do. I'm not a mercenary. I wanted to find you and rescue you."

All the frustration, fear and anger I've been trying to ignore suddenly bursts out at him. "Rescue me? I rescued you, remember? And now all you want is your reward? We should have left you there to incinerate."

"No, wait. Stop. Listen. Let me explain."

“There’s nothing to explain.” I’m shouting now. “I just want to get out of here. I just want to get away from you. I just want to know what’s going on. I just want to go home.” I’m shouting and trying not to cry. It’s all too much.

Caden reaches for my shoulder but I shake his hand off and keep walking.

“Sislie, no. Listen. It’s not about the reward. If it was, I’d go after the Queen’s money. She offered a reward too. Please, let me explain.”

A croaking bark interrupts him. We stop for a minute to let Gundega catch her breath. She coughs, pants, croaks again “Fae Queen. Don't trust her. She's the one who made me kidnap you.”

“What? Queen Maelys?” Suddenly, the confusion that plagued me in Gundega's cottage floods me again. “Why would the Queen of the Fae want to kidnap me when I’m supposed to be on my way to train with her?” I desperately want to get out of here and away from both of them.

“She said it was to keep you safe from the Raiders. That they wanted to capture the Queen-to-be and ransom you for land across the river from that Human village, First Bend.”

Caden interjects, “That's where I live, and my mother. But we've got to keep moving. There was still lots of smoke in that last exit tunnel and those others are getting closer.”

I cross my arms and plant both feet squarely on the ground. “I'm not going anywhere until I learn what in the hells is going on!”

“Please, Sislie, it's too dangerous here.”

“Listen to the boy,” Gundega croaks. “We’ll have time for explaining later.”

"Ok, but it better be soon." I'm so angry and frustrated, and this new information is overwhelming me with mistrust and confusion.

We hasten down the tunnel as fast as we can, often having to stoop through the dwarf-built passage. Caden takes Gundega's hand to help her keep her balance and go a bit faster. "We'd better hurry—I can tell now it's the Queen's Guards. I recognize them now from when they stopped me on the way out of town, and they're getting closer."

"Maybe they found traces of us in that cave where we were resting," I point out.

"Never mind, just go," Caden whispers, without stopping. "Wait, wait, up ahead on the right there's another passage to the surface."

We veer to the right, crouching and ducking as the exit passage narrows, trying not to choke on the dust and smoke. When we get to the exit tunnel, we crowd in and pull some debris and rocks down behind us. Gundega collapses on the ground, and sits, leaning against the wall. She feebly sketches an Unnoticeable spell in the air. The smoke and dust are choking, and she does her best to suppress a coughing fit.

"Sh, sh," Caden holds his hand up near her mouth. "They're almost here." We all hold our breath and hear the light but purposeful tread of the Queen's Guard as they make their way down the tunnel toward us. Gundega is turning red from trying not to cough, and I attempt to calm her breathing by resting my hands on her shoulders, ignoring my own chest burning from the smoke and dust. The Guards slow down when they near our exit, but luck is with us and the captain brusquely tells them to keep moving when he sees the debris, since some of these exits are unstable.

"Ok, they're gone," Caden says after a few minutes. "Let's open this up again." I make another ball of light, and we start to clear the debris we pulled down to hide us. But just as we glimpse the tunnel, one of the side walls collapses and a heap of rock and dirt falls, blocking our way out.

"Here, remember this?" Gundega pulls out the little shovel from her carrysack, that she and I used to rescue him from the fallen tree. We dig frantically, but the walls of the passage keep collapsing. Then a rock falls on Gundega's head, and she collapses. I fight the panic I'm feeling. We're trapped, and soon we won't be able to breathe.

Caden urges us to dig some more, but we don't get anywhere. He stops shoveling for a moment and puts his hand on my shoulder. "Sislie, you're a dancer. Can you *flicker*? Is it possible to *flicker* someone else with you? Could you *flicker* Gundega out to the main tunnel?" He sees my frown, but persists. "Could you *flicker* yourself out? Maybe with someone digging on the other side...."

"I'm not sure. I've only ever done the *flicker* as a dance move, and never from standing still."

I try to calculate the distance out to the center of the passage, but I'm filled with dread at the possibility of *flickering* into solid wall. I look at him and in the dim light I can see his eyes, brimming with hope and confidence. And warmth. It helps me remember the first time I ever tried to *flicker*, and how easy it turned out to be.

I take a deep breath. I *flicker*. There's an instant of panic, not knowing exactly where I'm going to land. But then suddenly, yes! I'm in the main passage. Heart pounding, I get to work pulling away rocks with my hands, and him digging the dirt on the other side. Between the two of us, we manage to clear an opening big enough to pull Gundega through, and Caden crawls out behind her.

"Are you ok?" I can't help but respond to those eyes. He's covered in dirt, but I hug him. And he hugs me back. It's nice. We contrive a sledge from her cloak and some branches, and pull her back to the cave where we last slept.

By the time we get there, I'm shaking with exhaustion. I sit down and take some deep breaths. I feel for the energy of the earth so I can replenish myself. And heal Gundega. She's weak from her injuries, but puts her hand up to stop me from the healing. "You young people should go on ahead. Just leave me with a waterskin and a few travel cakes, and I'll find my way out. They're not interested in me, Sislie, only you."

Caden goes to reply, but I interrupt him. "No, that's not going to happen. We're in this together, and we'll get us all out, no matter what."

CHAPTER 20

Baba rests on a large rock near the cave mouth, a crooked smile on her wrinkled face, as she watches the growing dragons tussle like enormous kittens in the clearing. They're now as big as mountain cougars. They have grown muscular and powerful, though they still retain a cat-like flexibility along their long bodies. She wonders how large they'll get. As they grow, their shape is changing too. Elongated necks have grown a spiky ridge, and their great wings have become more bat-like, looking like tough glossy leather. Their fangs are growing too. They hiss and snort through a mouthful of fearsome daggers as they tumble and play, chasing each other around the clearing.

She's convinced the hissing has got to be more than animal sounds. And surely the images she sees in her mind when they look at her with their swirling eyes are a form of communication, though she isn't clear about what it means.

They definitely seem to have some way of speaking with Minason, who is completely devoted to them. His unfaltering determination to satisfy their incessant hunger must mean they have somehow enchanted him. Shc idly wonders if there are more eggs somewhere on the mountain.

They can't stay here at the top of the mountain indefinitely. Eventually, villagers are sure to come across them. But as long as they're land bound, the dragons can't go far, awkward as they are on the ground.

She's been gathering extra provisions in case they have to move, during her increasingly sporadic trips down to the village—her hut now empty of bowls, cooking utensils and what few blankets and warm clothing she owns. Her sons, the Headman Brom and Minason's Da, don't miss her, uninterested in the comings and goings of an old woman. If they think about her at all, they'll assume she's at the women's lodge, or foraging for mushrooms or berries in the forest.

She watches the dragons waddle over to the hot crevasse that used to be Minason's cave, and stare down into its simmering depths. They do this every day, often more than once, fascinated by the smoke and fire. The grandmothers' myths about dragons had them eating a type of crunchy lava to feed their fire. They must be looking for that, though she can see nothing more than ruddy smoke.

Her lanky grandson comes hurrying down from the meadow on the other side of the peak, carrying three large grouse over his shoulder. Two for the dragons and one for himself and Baba to share. She loves the way he's become more sure of himself as he succeeds in bringing them game twice every day. He doesn't seem to mind racing up and down the mountain to do chores for his Da, and then hunt for the always ravenous dragons. He tosses them the two largest grouse, and they quickly devour them, then shamble to the mouth of their cave and curl up for a nap.

The larger dragon he has named Blaze. Richly hued in turquoise and silver, she has zig-zag markings up and down her now considerable length, similar to the pattern he first saw on her egg. The smaller one is lighter in color, with a silver ruff near the base of his long neck. Minason calls him Fancy. Baba wanted to give them more elaborate names in keeping with the mythic status of dragons, but they seem to respond to his names, so they stick to that.

Small animals on the mountain top are becoming more elusive to hunt as more and more of them recognize Minason as a danger. The land-bound Blaze and Fancy can't travel far, and are clumsy hunters. They know how to enchant prey into stillness by staring at them with their swirling eyes, but prefer to pounce while they are active, and so they usually miss. They largely rely on what Minason provides, nonchalantly accepting his dedication to their feeding.

Baba serves Minason a generous portion of their roasted grouse. "We should move across to the other side of the meadow. There's a bigger cave there, and they can learn to fly off that cliff."

He swallows his bite of meat, wiping a drop of fat from his chin. "But Baba, that might be dangerous."

"Creatures that fly know when they're ready. I don't think we need to worry about that. They're growing so fast you won't be able to keep up with their feeding much longer. Once they fly, they'll be able to hunt for themselves. That's what those long talons and sharp teeth are for."

His daily hike back to the village will be longer, but Minason sees the wisdom in her suggestion. After the dragons finish napping, they gather their belongings and carry them in two trips across the alpine meadow to their new encampment. The dragons shamble noisily beside them.

When Blaze sees the cliff, she gleefully runs to it, spreads her leathery wings, and leaps over the edge. Minason screams and they watch aghast as she plummets, frantically flapping her wings to no avail. Fancy roars and hisses, flapping his own wings and jumping up and down at the edge of the precipice. But just as she's about to crash into the craggy rocks below, she spreads her wings as wide as they'll go and catches the air. She flies. She swoops up away from the cliff, her powerful wings mounting the sky. Their beat steadies, and she soars around in circles, roaring with glee. She flies over the valley, sparkling in the sunlight. She swoops down towards them, inviting Fancy to join her. But he stays put, and after a few more circuits she comes in for a clumsy landing.

Minason and Baba laugh and clap their hands as she regains her solid footing and tucks her wings. But now she's hungry again. She stares at Minason in that way she has, so he runs off to hunt, hoping the snares he set will have caught their next meal.

Fancy stands at the edge of the cliff, staring into the vastness over the valley below. Blaze tries to push him off, but he balks, snarling at her and snapping his teeth.

For several days he watches her fly, opening his wings and flapping them as much as he can on the ground. Then finally he takes a running leap and spreads his wings, flapping hard, and catches the air just as she did. Blaze joins him and they fly circles over their encampment, both roaring with glee.

They fly farther afield. One day, Blaze lands in their encampment with a goat that she scooped from a steep meadow, blood dripping from its crushed carcass. She drops it at Minason's feet, then swaggers over to the cave mouth and flops down for her nap. Minason and Baba receive it gratefully, as though it were a gift from the gods. They feast on the roasted meat and lay out the remainder in strips to dry for later. After that the dragons feed themselves bigger game, and Minason doesn't need to hunt for them anymore.

Some days later, Blaze crouches down on her haunches, drawing herself as low as she can, and springs into the air. Her wings heave mightily, flapping once, twice, three times and she climbs the sky, roaring with delight. She banks around towards Fancy and bellows at him, urging him to do the same. But Fancy just snorts and waddles to the cliff edge, where he nonchalantly hurtles himself into the air as always.

Later, Minason sees Fancy trying to crouch and spring again and again, managing only a couple of wing flaps before jolting back to the hard packed dirt. He goes to approach Fancy after one of these failed attempts, but Baba chuckles and holds him back. "Leave him, he'll master it in time. His legs are strong, but his wings still need to grow."

This is the first happy summer Minason has ever known. The dragons are a continual delight. He watches them for hours, and again dreams of flying. His Baba never scolds him or hits him. She talks with him in a kind voice, and tells him everything she knows about his Fae mother, Mina. She tells him stories the women have preserved, from before she was born, when the Asmung prospered and the tribe was governed by the grandmothers.

And there's plenty to eat. Berries, small game, mushrooms, and vegetables for tasty stews. The water on this side of the mountain has less of that sour, rank smell, and the air doesn't have the acrid taste that the village always leaves on his tongue. He has some color in his cheeks and looks more robust. They sleep on comfortable pallets they made for themselves in the cave, on beds of leaves and grasses, and blankets they brought from the village.

He figures out how to flatten pieces of birch bark by soaking them in hot water, then laying them flat to dry in the sun with stones holding down the edges. He draws many pictures of the dragons, his Baba, and the animals that inhabit Dragon's End Mountain. He still has to go down to the village every day to bring food and do chores for his Da, but he hardly notices his son's absences, and Minason manages to avoid him and his fists most of the time.

One quiet afternoon, he's contentedly sketching on a piece of birch bark when Blaze waddles over to him. She looms over him and stares, her golden eyes whirling. At the same time, he gets a picture of a grouse in his mind, and leaps up to go hunting for his dragons. *Wait a minute, she hunts for herself now. She's talking to me. This is her way of talking.* He realizes that's how she used to let him know when she was hungry. Minason laughs with delight. He pictures a badger and tries sending the image to Blaze. She snorts and shakes her head, showing her teeth, and sends him a picture of a small goat. They send pictures back and forth until Blaze tires of the game and flies off to hunt for her next meal.

Over the next days they convey many images to each other, mostly of animals and birds. They can't do it for very long, because Minason gets a sharp pain in his forehead just above his eyes if they do. They invite Fancy to join in their game, but he is less interested.

Another day, he hears a sound in his head. <<*MMEEENN-SS-SAAN*>> He looks up at Blaze, who transmits an image of a lanky youth with fair hair. It takes him a moment to recognize it as himself. He sends back an image of Blaze flying and gleaming in the sunlight. He says "Blaze," and this time the sound in his head is <<*VVV-LAYYZZ.*>> Minason giggles and dances up and down, ignoring the stabbing pain in his forehead.

He happily shares this new development with his Baba. She recalls, "There was another wall at the ruin I showed you. Part of it was still standing before the last earthshake. It had a picture of an enormous dragon with someone standing facing it, and a shadowy image above their heads. It was full of cracks, and we could never quite make it out, but it may have been a Fae. I always wondered if it was some kind of communication."

CHAPTER 21

One day Minason ventures farther than usual on the Asmung hunters' side of the mountain, looking for a bighorn sheep he's been wanting to draw. Just as he's settling down on a ledge near where he last saw the sheep, a couple of hunters emerge from the trail in search of the same sheep for prey. One of the hunters spots him ducking down behind an outcropping, and grabs him, casually slapping him and demanding to know what he's doing there. They search him and seize the small picture of the dragons he wears hanging from a string around his neck. Laughing at what an idiot he is, they march him down to the encampment where his uncle and the other hunters are sitting around their campfire, drinking hooch.

"What's this you've been wasting your time on, nephew?" the Headman demands when he sees the drawing.

"Um, I like to watch the animals and birds, Uncle Brom." Minason is good at evading his Da and uncle, but not at lying outright. "I... I like the salamanders and imagine what they'd look like with wings. I made it up, Uncle, honest."

Brom cuffs him and sends him sprawling on the ground. "Don't lie to me, I'm not your Da, that anyone can fool. Tell me what these are."

Minason is used to his Da's casual beatings, but he's seen the terrible injuries his brawny uncle can inflict with his fists and his feet, even when he's not really mad. Quaking, he submits. "Dragons, sir. They're dragons. There were eggs and they hatched after the earth shake, and my cave at the top split apart and it was hot, and Baba said they are dragons and they're real. They're beautiful and silver and blue. They're real, not just scary monster stories."

The hunters jeer and guffaw, urging the Headman to beat the truth out of him. But Headman Brom stays his hand. Minason is his only nephew and is not known as a liar. He has no sons of his own and is fond of the boy, in spite of his quirky behavior and half-Fae appearance. He had liked that skinny Fae girl, Mina, too, and regretted that he never got a child off her. "You'll bring us to their lair tomorrow. I'd like to taste their meat." He sticks out his brawny chest, smiling. "Blue skin you say? That'll make me a fine cloak."

Minason can't escape or outrun the hunters that surround him on the way back to the village, so he doesn't even try, enduring their taunts and shoves on the way down the mountain. When they get there, his Da beats him for being a liar and for hiding game from the hunters.

Bruised and despondent, he almost panics when his uncle sets a guard at his Da's door so he can't run away. But when he sees who his uncle has assigned to guard duty, he gets an idea.

That night Minason waits until he hears Da snoring. With furtive care, he tiptoes to the crock of fermented brew his Da thinks he doesn't know about, hidden in a corner of their hut. He takes his Da's big cup and slowly as he can, pours a cup of the hooch, flinching every time he hears a gurgle from the mouth of the crock. He sneaks it out to the guard, who gratefully accepts the relief from boring duty, not asking where it came from. He gulps it down, and Minason brings more, ever careful not to make any noise. The guard eventually drinks enough of the strong hooch to nod off.

Minason gathers what few belongings he can call his own, then sidles out of the hut past the guard, whose snoring is now almost as loud as his Da's.

He races back up the mountain in the dark. His keen night vision, a gift from his mother's Fae heritage, normally gives him the ability to discern the trees and animals of the natural world. But tonight, he flinches at every shadow. Nocturnal animal sounds that would usually intrigue him sound like hunters tracking him up the mountain. The hoot of an owl almost makes him fall off the bridge he made over that crevasse after the mountain shook.

Baba is waiting for him. When he didn't come back that night, she filled a couple of carrysacks with their belongings, food and water skins. The dragons are sleeping soundly, deep in the cave. They occasionally snort, projecting random dream pictures of flying, or diving down on an unsuspecting goat or deer on the slope of the mountain.

Minason has never had to wake the dragons. He tiptoes toward them, not knowing how they'll react. He doesn't want to touch them, cautious of their enormous teeth and talons. Instead, he calls their names softly, and sends them pictures of a sunny meadow full of rabbits and grazing deer.

Blaze wakes instantly. She casts her gaze on Minason, poised to flee near the opening of the cave. She looks at him placidly, golden eyes whirling.

He tries to convey the danger, sending a picture of hunters throwing spears that pierce dragon flesh. And another image of himself and Baba hurrying down the mountain trail with their belongings on their backs. Blaze nudges Fancy, who wakes up hissing and flashing his teeth. The dragons exit the cave unhurriedly and fly off into the night. Minason and Baba gather up their belongings and hurry down the mountain trail with as much as they can carry.

The next day, the hunters almost chase them down. Minason's keen hearing gives them enough warning to hide in an old giant fir with large roots and a cleft at its base. He tucks Baba into the deepest corner, frantically pulling branches in front of the opening. He crawls in beside her, tucking their carrysacks beside them and pulling the branches as close as he can before the hunters get close enough to detect them.

They wait breathlessly, keeping silent as the hunters approach their hiding place, arguing with each other about whether there really are such creatures as dragons, and whether or not their Headman is being gullible. Their search is perfunctory, distracted by the debate, and they soon decide the cowardly Minason wouldn't have gone this far. They return up the trail to more familiar grounds, declaring that they'll beat the crap out of him when they find him, for causing so much trouble.

Once the hunters have moved beyond hearing, Minason and Baba crawl out of their cramped hiding place and pull out their carrysacks. They hurry back to the trail and make their way down the mountain for several days, taking turns to sleep and keep watch. They remain wary, alert for any further sign of the hunters, who hopefully by now are satisfied to search in the other direction, in their habitual hunting grounds, since they're unaccustomed to venturing farther afield.

When they arrive at the base of Dragon's End Mountain, they don't know which way to go. The valley they had only seen from their cliff's edge seems much wider than it had appeared from above, and there's little shelter. They decide to stick to the forested path around its long edge and set out. But Blaze lands with a flapping of her great wings and blocks their way. She nudges them with her snout and sends pictures of a clearing similar to the one they abandoned on Dragon's End.

They turn in the other direction, traversing the narrow edge of the valley, following a well-worn path which soon rises up the slope of the adjacent mountain. It's easy to follow and not too steep, so they make good time. They don't see much of the dragons because the trees on either side don't give enough room for them to land, but they catch occasional glimpses between the tops of trees.

After three days of climbing, they arrive at a small clearing about halfway up the mountain. The dragons light down beside them, but not to rest this time. Blaze stares at Minason with her golden eyes and sends him an image of silvery objects darting around in a blue, shimmering background. She turns to force her way through the undergrowth. Ever more enormous and powerful, but still ungainly on the ground, she pushes through to a small plateau overlooking the valley.

Minason and Baba look around the clearing. They put down their carrysacks and breathe in the sweet air. A glistening stream of clean water flows into a pool with lots of fish, just as Blaze had shown him. It's far enough off the main trail that they can avoid any Humans or Fae who live or hunt in the area, and the rock shelf is big enough for the dragons to land and take off comfortably. The cave has no sign of recent use. It's not as big as the one they had on Dragon's End, but it's dry and has the clean loamy smell of the mountain forest. There's enough room for both them and the dragons.

Minason goes to the pool, to see if he can catch a fish or two for their supper while Baba gathers grasses for their new sleeping pallets. He lies down on his belly at the edge of the pool, smiling to himself, with his arms in the chilly mountain water. He waits, still and patient, until a fish approaches to inspect his slowly wiggling fingers. He snags it with his quick hands. Then another. He brings them back for a delicious and untainted meal to share with Baba in their new home. Blaze and Fancy have already taken off to explore their new hunting ground.

They rarely see anyone on the mountain, and avoid them when they do. The few Fae that pass by may be aware of them, but as always, they disdain contact with anyone not their own kind. But one day Minason overhears a couple of Rangers conversing on the same trail that brought them to their new home. They call this place Cougar Mountain.

They are finally safe.

CHAPTER 22

A bent and cloaked figure scuttles into the parlor and bows obsequiously to the Queen, glancing at the silent Lord Jarin standing beside her. His skin is leathered, his wide mouth and flattened nose give his face a slight resemblance to the chameleon staring at him from its gilded cage at her feet. His furtive eyes reveal a pale violet, the sure sign of one who carries a Fae bloodline. But he's a broken Fae, prematurely aged, looking more like an elderly Human than Fae.

Her thin lips form a faint smile as her spy kneels on the dais at her feet, and she takes a sweet cake from the platter at her elbow, holding it for a moment before she reaches forward to give it to him. "What have you learned for your Queen, little toad?"

"Thank you, Your Magnificence, I have much to tell." His voice is soft, high pitched, breathy, fawning. He licks his lips and longingly eyes the sweet cake in his hand, but sets it aside without taking a bite. "There is a forest fire on Cougar Mountain, where that Gundega was holding on to young Sislie for you. Her cottage has burned down and there's no trace of them. My informant among the Raiders reports that they probably perished in the fire."

“Fire? Was there lightning on the mountain?”

“They didn't say so, Splendid One, but I believe the Raiders started it themselves. They still sneak onto our side of the peninsula, but they’re poor hunters. They sometimes use fire to chase their prey toward archers hidden in their blinds. This time it got out of control.”

“Never mind, the rains are coming soon, and that will take care of the fire.” She muses out loud to herself, “If the girl is dead, who is the next suitable candidate? It can’t be from the Hummingbird Clan. They’ve already given their two.”

“Maybe Lord Jarin’s niece ....”

Her look silences him. “If I want your opinion, I'll ask for it.”

“Humbly sorry, Majesty,” and he bows even deeper, forehead on his knees.

Queen Maelys leans her head back on her throne, thinking or dozing. Ned can neither move nor speak until she permits it. She wakes with a small start, and scolds, “Are you going to keep me waiting forever? What's the rest of your report?”

“Your Highness, two enormous birds have been seen over Dragon's End Mountain. They’re not normal birds. They are said to be bright blue and silver, and shiny.” He spreads his arms wide, and his attempt to rise is squelched by a sharp glance from the Queen. “I've never seen them myself, but my informant tells me the larger of the two is as big as a horse. They live somewhere on Dragon's End Mountain. A half-Fae lad from that Asmung village apparently tends them. But they fly farther than Dragon's End. There have been sightings at First Bend, and at Clan holdings on Cougar Mountain.”

Her eyes narrow as he speaks, and take on a hard gleam. She glances around at the luminous tapestries on the walls and points at one of them. "Look there, little toad. Look carefully at the tapestry and tell me what you see."

He stumbles off the dais, almost stepping on his precious sweet cake, and scurries to the tapestry she's pointing to. The Queen raises her hand and traces a looping figure in the air. The tapestry comes alive with pictures of giants and fantastic beasts battling, some of them flying and breathing fire. They're immense, shining bright in silver, turquoise, bright red, and purple. Their enormous bodies are shaped similar to the glittering long necked salamander that crouches in the golden cage at her side, but the beating of their tremendous wings eclipses everything in Ned's imagination as he beholds, mouth gaping.

"These are the dragons of old. Go. Find those birds. See them with your own eyes. I need to know if those large birds are the same. Tell no one."

Neither they nor the silent Jarin hear the sharp intake of breath behind a spyhole in the wall at the side of her throne. Nor the quiet footsteps as Liana's feet hurry away.

Her voice is even more shrill than usual. "Get these off me, you lazy slatterns. I haven't got all day. I'm tired. I need my nap," she scolds the handmaidens painstakingly divesting her of the headpiece and court gown.

Liana helps her into her silken feathered robe as the other handmaidens deliver the court attire to the Queen's dressing room. They pull back the bedclothes from her canopied bed, placing the golden salamander cage at its foot.

"Get out." She waves them away, turning to her bed, but as soon as they're out of her bedchamber, she hurries to the door and places a small ornate bar across it to block anyone from entering. Then, her spindly body quivering with excitement, she pulls a small latch hidden behind a tapestry, sketching an angular figure in the air with her other hand.

A small door springs open to reveal a narrow cupboard lined with silver and known only to her. She eagerly snatches four ancient scrolls from the cupboard and brings them to her night table, where she unrolls the first two and tosses them on her bed after a cursory inspection.

But the third scroll draws her attention, and she slowly pores over the ancient text. Maelys remembers some of it from her early days as an idealistic young Queen, nearly three hundred years ago, when she was learning to govern and had care for the Land. But now, all she cares about is the passage describing how the dragons of ancient times, in return for a favor from the dryads, bestowed on them a drop of their blood. In this way, the Fae came into being, with the gift of enchantments, their highly sensitive wings, long life, and intelligence with which to rule the Land. Whether this was an account of actual events or a myth was never clear. But the Fae accept it as true, and venerate the memory of dragons.

She pores over the scroll a second time, muttering to herself and feverishly searching for more about the blood.

A drop of blood… just a drop… long life… it has to … even immortality….

She grabs another scroll, this time searching for references to the elixir of TAN, the last god, sleeping in the grotto as she waits for the newly anointed Queen.

Power… power to rule… more elixir… surely more power… power to triumph… it has to be….

There's nothing more in the scrolls. She sweeps them all off her bed onto the carpet, and, intoxicated with dreams of eternal life and eternal power, she sinks down to her pillow and closes her eyes.

It should be mine… it's mine… the elixir… and the blood… powerful blood… immortal blood… surely immortal… powerful… young again... beautiful... need a dragon… mine… it's mine… live... forever….

Liana silently closes the cover to her spyhole in the unused servants' passage behind the Queen's apartment, frustrated that she couldn't hear what the Queen was muttering to herself. But as she hurries down the secret passage, she repeats to herself the elements of the spell that Maelys sketched over the secret cupboard.

CHAPTER 23

“I’m sure it was her essence, Torin. It was only a trace, but it was definitely Sislie.” Lady Nerysa paces around their spacious drawing room overlooking the treetops of Hummingbird Village. A powerful healer, she’s been using her sensing ability to quest for her beloved daughter every day.

“I hope so, my love.” Lord Torin turns to answer a hail from the door of their chalet. He comes back carrying a scroll, a glimmer of hope in his eyes, the first since their daughter disappeared. “This is from Kairon. He says the Queen’s Guard have found evidence of her in the dwarf tunnels of Cougar Mountain.”

“The abandoned dwarf tunnels. I wonder how she could have got in there.”

“Apparently she’s not alone. But hardly anyone knows about them, and the entrances were hidden ages ago. Remember, the ancestors made a covenant to leave them alone.”

She frowns, reaching for the memory. “What do you make of that rumor that time goes missing for anyone who enters without permission?”

“It seems unlikely, but the dwarves did leave many mysteries behind.”

"If she's in there, it explains why the seekers haven't been able to find her. I wonder if she's been in there this whole time."

"Kairon says the Guard are expecting to escort her to Queensdale. He asks that we join him there to greet her."

Nerysa is already turning to fetch her travel cloak.

CHAPTER 24

Gundega snores quietly, curled up at the edge of the cave, wrapped in her orange cape, occasionally muttering. The little cat is snuggled under her chin. Without her usual severe demeanor, she looks almost soft as she sighs and turns over. I watch her sleep, asking myself why I don't hate her. How could I become fond of this woman who kidnapped me and treated me with harsh indifference all those weeks? But I have. It's not part of being a healer, because I don't necessarily like everyone I help. But the story she told has stirred a deep place in me, and I feel a pity and sorrow I've never experienced.

Never could I have imagined the tragic plight of a child taken from her home and made to serve a debased tribe, poisoned by the toxic land and water of Dragon's End Mountain.

My parents had told me about how they and other Clan healers went to offer remedies and help to the Asmung, and relocation to a safer place. But what had been their taciturn pride in the past had turned to mistrustful hostility, and their leaders, now all men, refused to accept help or even acknowledge the need for help.

I wonder what became of the baby that Mina gave birth to, that caused her terrible death.

Gundega wraps her cloak closer around herself and the little cat purrs and snuggles deeper.

I can barely make out Caden. He sits leaning against the wall by the tunnel opening, his eyes closed. I can't tell if he's asleep or keeping vigil with his distance sensing. I wonder about him too. I keep being distracted by his exotic half-Human beauty, his muscular build and the invitation in his eyes that he doesn't try to hide. I try to ignore the warm shiver that rises from under my belly as I watch him.

The air is stale, but at least there's no smoke and we've stopped coughing. I'm exhausted but restless. The thoughts and pictures in my mind won't stop spinning. I get up and walk over to the pool, keeping my ball of light small. I can't tell where it's flowing from but the water is clear and fresh.

I slip off my cloak and untie the string holding my shift, letting it fall to the ground. I kick off my shoes and slide in. The water is shockingly cold but glorious, and I splash like an otter, letting it cleanse my body and clear my mind. The effects of the sleeping powder have nearly worn off, though there are still many gaps in my memory.

I duck under and dive into the center. There's a faint radiance at the bottom, which is quite a bit further down than I thought it would be. On my third dive, I touch bottom. The glow is coming from a pale green stone about the size of my palm. My hand reaches out of its own accord and I pick it up. I bring it to the surface and feel its slight warmth. I hold it in both hands, gazing at it.

I'm so unaccountably happy to have found this stone that I don't immediately notice Caden staring at me with gleaming eyes. He grins but looks away, and I hurriedly put my clothes back on over my shivering skin. I tuck the stone into the pocket of my cloak. I'm blushing, and my wing nubs are tingling, but I turn my back to him and walk over to the wall of elven runes. I try to concentrate on seeing through their glamour, but my tingling body is distracting me. The glyphs are no less elusive than they were before.

I sidle over to where Gundega and the cat are sleeping, pretending I don't see Caden still sitting near the tunnel entrance with his eyes closed again. I flop down near Gundega and the cat and drop into the soft abyss of sleep.

I have no idea how long we sleep. When I wake up, Gundega has refilled the water skins and we share our dwindling supply of travel cakes. Caden and I both blush when we look at each other, but then turn away, only to glance again. We gather our meagre possessions and head out the way we were going.

How long have we been here? Was it yesterday? Last week? I have no idea. The uniform dark of the tunnels has removed any sense of the passage of days, and there's a weird but palpable feeling of time lost.

Gundega refuses the sledge but lets Caden pick up her carrysack. Caden reports that the Queen's Guards have left the vicinity, and we trudge to the next exit, the little cat riding jauntily on his shoulder. The first exit tunnel is blocked, as is the one after, and we carefully skirt past the collapsed exit that trapped us. Finally, after three more exits that don't seem to go anywhere, Gundega staggering and leaning on Caden, we emerge through a thicket covering the opening of the last exit tunnel.

The air is clear and surprisingly, there are spring blossoms on the ground and the sun is warm on our faces. Surely it can't be spring already. But snowdrops and crocuses snuggle against the wall beside our exit. We're on a broad ledge, more like a clearing covered in grasses and fresh shoots, and surrounded by tall pines. The mountain falls away down a steep cliff. A wide valley is visible below, and we can see another mountain on the other side. Caden helps Gundega to a rock shelter where she sinks down and closes her eyes. He wanders off to explore the clearing.

I'm worried about Gundega. My heartfire draws me to her and I sit down behind her. I take her head in my hands. I *feel* into her, probing her injuries and checking her all over. Her broken leg is healed, but the sprained knee is healing more slowly than it should, and she's drained and exhausted from our long time in the tunnels, and the constant fear. I try to reach down for earth energy to boost her strength, but I'm exhausted too, still not fully recovered from all the weeks of sleeping powder and inactivity. I remember I should replenish myself first, before healing someone else, and begin to draw up some healing earth energy to fortify my reserves.

All of a sudden, the mountain shudders and a deafening crack splits the air. A flock of crows explodes out of the tree beside us. A ledge of rock at the edge of our clearing crumbles and cascades down the cliff, pulling a small tree down with it. Across the valley, reddish smoke is geysering out of the top of the mountain, forming a great black cloud.

Caden rushes over to where we were sitting. Gundega is sprawled on the ground. She's panting, but nothing has fallen on her and she seems ok.

"We'll have to stay here. It's the safest place for us right now." He speaks from his Ranger training. "Just stay away from the edge and don't go back to the tunnel opening in case it collapses."

We're too tired and shocked to argue, and besides, there's no place to go.

After a while, the birds flutter back down into their tree. There's another slight tremor, but not enough to shake out the birds again. Through an opening in the pines, we can see more ruddy smoke belching from the top of the mountain and spreading out across the sky. Gundega sits up and points, "that's Dragon's End Mountain. It's supposed to be an extinct volcano."

"No, it isn't." Caden drops his carrysack and bow on a grassy mound and looks again. "Or maybe it is. I've never seen it from this angle."

The sun has retreated behind the smoke clouds, and the air is suddenly chilly. He gathers branches to build a lean-to away from the rock slope. I'm still tired, but the earthshake has jolted me awake and I feel agitated. I start to pace the scrubby clearing. We should take time to rest and recover, but all the questions come back and pile up, and I'm feeling mad again. And that stuff about the Queen has me more confused than ever.

"Come and shelter," he beckons me to the lean-to, "We should be safe to stay here for a couple of days. Hopefully, there will be no more shakes. You should rest, Sislie."

Suddenly those eyes are not enticing any more, and the inviting smile on his face just annoys me. I need answers, and I need them now. "Sit. Explain." The only earthshake danger right now is coming from me.

He looks startled, but comes to sit on a boulder close to me. "Like I said, I saw you in a dream. It was more like a vision. You were glowing and twirling, your wings..."

"You were spying on me?" I'm shouting, sick and tired of being confused.

"No, No. It was a vision. I wanted to rescue you. I still want to rescue you."

"Don't be stupid. We rescued you. Remember? From under the tree? Or was that just a ploy?"

"No, don't you be stupid. That's not possible. I was looking for you. I had seen a cottage, maybe Gundega's cottage. I mean, not in the vision, but another time when I was out on patrol. I was heading there when I got trapped by the fire. I wasn't there for the reward, believe me."

He looks at me with such pleading, violet eyes glowing and wanting. I almost burst out laughing, but just a nervous snicker escapes me. He looks shocked, hurt. But he carries on. "A Trader in my village—I'm from First Bend—said you had disappeared, and the Hummingbird Clan is desperate to find you. They offered a reward for your safe return, or even information of your fate."

"So you are just after the reward." My hand snakes forward to slap his lying face but he catches my wrist before I can connect.

"Sislie, I'm a Ranger. We go on rescue missions. It's our job. It started as an adventure, but Sislie, believe me. As soon as I heard about you, I had this urge to find you. And I had this dream. You were so beautiful."

His eyes, those eyes. I try to look away from them, but my eyes slide down to his soft lips. I start to melt. I lean back and steel myself. "So what about the Queen?"

"That's the weird part. She intercepted me on my way out of town just as I was leaving to find you. She knew things about me, said she had a duty for me, a quest. She said you had been kidnapped and offered a double reward if I would bring you to her."

I plop down on the ground beside him, my head reeling from this new information on top of the exhaustion and fear. "So, what do you intend?"

He sits across from me, keeping a respectful distance. "I'm a hunter, Sislie, and a seeker. I know when a trail is false, and her offer had duplicity painted all over it."

"Damn right it's false." The gravelly comment from an apparently sleeping Gundega. Eyes still closed, she continues, "She tricked me into believing the Raiders were going to kidnap you for ransom. She said I should keep you safe until she sent word. But she didn't send word. She only sent those ruffians to take you."

"But Gundega, why the sleeping powder?"

"She gave it to me, said you're strong and willful, and could *flicker* away at any time. That's why the sleeping powder. To keep you docile." She looks at me, her face twisted in a mixture of shame and defiance. "I've never used it before and I think I gave you too much. I think that's what wiped out your memory."

I look back at her. She was my jailer all those weeks. I have hated her, but I have healed her. It's my duty. And she saved me from the forest fire. Also I have heard her story and seen into her gruff innocence. So I can't just hate her. I can't love her either, but that tiny ember of affection stirs in me.

She rolls onto her side. "We need to go soon." But she sinks down into herself, spent, asleep almost instantly.

I kneel at her head and place my hands at the sides of her weathered cheeks, *feeling* for her signature life force that will tell me the state of her wellness. The wound on her forehead is almost healed, as is her broken leg, though her knee is swollen again. She's going to be alright, but she's completely worn out. I have nothing of my own reserves to give her, but reach down for earth energy. I draw up as much as I can for her, and also for myself. I'm still tired, but feel stronger and somewhat reassured. Caden is exploring the plateau for more hidden rations or tools, but all he finds is an empty waterskin and a torn rag of grey cloth. After I'm finished with Gundega, the healer in me calls to him. "I need to check your injuries from the tree fall."

"I'm fine," but he comes closer and sits at my bidding.

I cradle his face in my hands and measure his wellness as sufficient. His arm is mostly healed, and there are no other injuries. He's young and healthy and strong, and I'm aware of how close he is, and how attractive. He leans toward me, eyes inviting, lips soft. But I'm in healer mode now, and gently push him away—though our eyes meet and a thrill of heat flares through my body.

CHAPTER 25

"Gracious Majesty, I have not sighted them with my own eyes, but all descriptions of the flying creatures are like the dragons you showed me in the tapestry. Both of them are silver and turquoise, and one of them has a ruff around its neck." At her nod, Ned bows and scuttles backwards out of the morning room.

Maelys calls for her handmaidens to dress her. She's in a fine mood, almost pleasant, and hardly scolds, humming to herself and muttering about pretty salamanders. There is a bounce in her step when Kairon escorts her to the throne room and up onto her dais, and she even acknowledges his assistance. She takes her throne and the courtiers all sigh with relief when she smiles.

"This day I have a special proclamation." She turns to her Lord Chamberlain Jarin, who hastily signals at the scribe to record her words. "An unusual species of flying salamander has been seen in my Queendom. There are two. I would have them for my Royal menagerie."

The babble that ensues is against all protocol but the Queen lets it continue for a few moments, smiling to herself and taking a sip of the hibiscus mead always sitting on a small ornate table by her side. She raises her hand, and the chatter is cut off. Her usually unpleasant voice is almost purring. "Whoever brings me one or both will be richly rewarded, no matter who they are."

Kairon and Jarin exchange glances. They usually work in opposition to each other, but for once neither of them knows what this is about. The Royal menagerie is just a hobby, where Maelys collects interesting creatures, mostly gifts from the coaxer Clans who know how to charm and entice birds and animals into unusual shapes and colors, sometimes even combining different species. But why would creatures for the menagerie be important enough to warrant a royal proclamation?

She summons the Captain of her Guards, who kneels before her. "Attican, you will take your best and most capable Guards. You will find these creatures, and you'll bring them to me."

Kairon is loath to contradict her directly and chooses his words with care. "Splendid Majesty, preparations for the Grand Conclave are well underway and Queen-to-be Sislie has yet to be found. I wonder if that could be made a priority."

"Yes, of course, both."

Later, she summons Attican to her private drawing room. She bids him join her on the settee next to her and dredges up a remnant of charm. "Dear faithful Attican, once again I trust you to keep a secret for your Queen. Take only your most discreet Guards back to the dwarf tunnels, the ones who know how to keep silence."

He nods and watches her with cautious eyes, hoping his vow to his Queen won't again require him to do things against the best interests of the Land.

"Young Sislie is important, of course. But the flying creatures are more so. The others don't realize. They're not mere salamanders, but dragons. Returned to us from the time before remembering." She ignores his astonished gape and taps the back of his hand with her sharp fingernail, her voice and eyes taking on more of their usual hardness. "I must have one. I must have one above all other things. If you sight one, you will drop all other pursuits and find it and bring it to me. Both would be better."

She smiles again and pats him on the cheek, sending him on his way. Attican can scarce believe this incredible news. But surely not dragons. They are creatures of myth. And even if they were real, why would she want them for the Royal menagerie?

She watches him bow and leave her drawing room. He is a loyal and capable retainer, but he is only one. The proclamation will go out to all the Clans, all the towns, to the seaport and villages down the coast. Even to the Raiders. She will have her dragons. She will have their blood. She will live forever.

Chance of the Rocky Shores listens to the courier's message with care. The Queen's proclamation specifically says no matter who brings in the flying salamanders, they'll receive a lavish reward. Surely that's an oblique reference to the Shorelanders.

He immediately starts making preparations, calling Pokum to open the weapons locker and gather their best hunters. The Queen will have her flying salamander. His people will have their land across from First Bend.

CHAPTER 26

Caden has fashioned a lean-to big enough to shelter all three of us. We've decided to stay and rest for a couple of days before heading down the mountain. He builds a fire pit and snares a rabbit for Gundega and him to eat. I make do with one of our few remaining travel cakes, supplemented by some nuts and dried berries that survived the winter on our plateau. I'm hungry but I still can't bring myself to eat animal flesh.

Caden has many useful skills for living in the wild. He busies himself finding a stream where we can fill our water skins, and forages nuts and berries and some edible mushrooms. He devises a cooking bowl out of the peeled bark of birch trees and cooks a stew with edibles from down the steep path at the side of our plateau. Gundega inspects the food he brings without comment, hobbling around with her walking stick and finding roots and herbs to add to the stew.

I can't help it. I like the look of him. I keep glancing at him, enjoying the aliveness I feel after all those weeks of dull lethargy. He keeps glancing at me, too. I imagine what it would be like to have his arms around me, but I'm still not sure if I can trust him. Or myself.

She sets Unnoticeable wards each night so we can sleep undisturbed. There's not much smoke after a cool rain, but that night I can't sleep. It's too crowded to toss and turn, and now I remember I'm supposed to get training for the Grand Conclave where I'll be anointed as the new Queen. I'm worried. If it's already spring, that's coming all too soon.

I sink into a murky twilight, bitterness and frustration boiling up again as I hear the voices from my dreams raised in anger. *You've got to do this. There is no other option... no other option... no other option.* I press closer to the corner and sob into the crook of my arm, hoping nobody will hear me. The little cat snuggles up against my belly, and finally I descend into restless sleep, full of memories of the maelstrom that was my life all last summer. I dream. My cousin Marielle setting out for her initiation at Queensdale. My mother sobbing that she's been killed. Dancing in my glade. Fear. Anger. Fire. Smoldering eyes. Caden. In my dream, I reach toward him, I melt into him, I kiss him, I fall into a deep sleep.

A comforting scent penetrates my dream as I drift awake. Something precious, warm, safe, enfolds me for a moment before I realize where I am. I startle the rest of the way awake. It's my mother questing for me. I can almost hear her calling my name. *Sislie, Sislie.* Awareness of her floods my consciousness, and with it, the jolting awareness of my urgent duty.

As I start to stir, the little cat leaps up from where it was sleeping and jumps on me. Then it jumps on Caden, who's on his feet instantly awake and orders us to grab our belongings. "The Queen's Guard are in the tunnels again, and they're almost here." He helps Gundega to her feet and we scramble to the path at the edge of our clearing, just as their determined footsteps stop at our exit.

"They're here." A shouted command. "Stop her before they get away."

The six tall uniforms burst into our clearing. They're all warriors, all armed with swords and bows, and stern expressions.

"Get your hands off me!" They disarm Caden before he can draw his bow, pulling his arms behind his back and starting to tie them.

Gundega kicks and tries to hit them with her little shovel, but they fend her off easily.

Their leader grabs me by the shoulder. I could *flicker* away, but where? Off the cliff edge? Once again, I'm somewhere I don't know. I pull myself up as tall as I can, trying to rally as much presence as a reluctant Queen-to-be can dredge up out of the remains of my dignity.

"Let go of me! Get your hands off us!" I yell, my voice unable to hide the quiver of fear threatening to shake me apart. "These are my guides and companions, and are to be treated with honor."

Their leader releases my shoulder and bows to me, but he is implacable. "Your Grace, I am Attican, captain of the Queen's Guard. You must come with us. Her Majesty Queen Maelys has sent us to escort you safely to Queensdale Palace. Your companions may come too and they'll be safe as well, as long as they don't try to interfere."

I don't have an answer for this. It's the Queen who ordered my kidnapping, but it's the Queen I'm supposed to go to for my training, and it's the Queen I'm supposed to become. And there's no escape from these warriors.

Suddenly, the crows squawk loudly and burst out of their pine tree at the edge of the clearing. There is a great swoop of wings and an astonishing creature dives down from the sky, landing near the edge of the cliff. Shining silver and turquoise, it's enormous, bigger than a bear. No coaxer could conjure such a one out of their profuse imagination. Its body looks like an immense salamander with a sparkling ruff around its long neck. Just as it tucks its huge wings and takes a couple of awkward steps toward us, another great swoop brings a second, even bigger creature plummeting out of the sky. This one has bright turquoise and silver blazing along its body. It lands near its fellow and turns swirling golden eyes on us.

I'm unable to move. All my mind knows is that I'm prey. I have no will, and nowhere to run or hide. Out of the corner of my eye, I see Gundega and Caden also paralyzed. The Guards too.

We all stand, passive as tree stumps as they waddle close and sniff us all over. A tiny corner of my brain registers that we've been glamoured, and is amazed. When the first giant salamander is inspecting me, I catch a whiff of loamy forest with a trace of cinnamon. It reminds me of the apothecary in my Clan village. They take their time, paying closest attention to faces, hands and crotches.

Finished with its examination, the larger one turns away, knocking over the Captain of the Guard with its long tail. Unable to move, he lies on his back, staring with wide eyes. It hisses and snorts, and nudges the other creature with its snout. The one with the ruff also turns away, this time knocking Caden over. Then they abruptly crouch on their great haunches and spring upward, vaulting into the smoky sky.

I'm not a meal after all. I breathe a sigh of relief, but I still can't move. After what seems like a long time, the crows return, but, noticing that we're not moving, they first light down in our encampment to look for food. One of them purloins a travel cake Gundega had just taken from her carrysack when the Guards found us. They gradually return to their branches.

The smoky sun is approaching midday when I start to feel some sensation in my hands and feet. I wiggle my fingers, and find I can turn my head. Everyone else is still motionless, but then Attican, the captain, rolls over and gets up off the ground, groping for his sword. Soon everyone is moving around, looking at each other without speaking.

One of the Guards is the first to find his voice. "Captain, it's dragons, just like we were told to watch out for. The Queen..."

"Yes. Dragons. Queen." The captain barks, "We abandon all pursuits if we see dragons, and above all else, we must capture one and deliver it to her Majesty." He turns to me and bows. "Begging your pardon, Your Grace, but we must leave you to make your own way down the mountain to Queensdale with all haste. It's very important that you report to her Majesty as soon as possible. We have an important mission from the Queen, that takes priority over all others."

I can't believe what I just heard. Dragons? Capture? "No! Wait! That's wrong!"

He ignores my shout and on his command, the Guards gather near him as he sketches an angular enchantment in the air with both hands, and speaks the buzzing words that will open a portal. They all step as one through the opening that appears, and vanish.

We're left standing on a cliff at the edge of Cougar Mountain, stupefied. Caden is the first to speak. "I've heard rumors. A couple of the Rangers have seen enormous shining birds over Dragon's End, but nobody knew what they were, and these are much bigger than described. But dragons, they can't be real. They're creatures of legend."

"Dragons are not just legend. They're central to the ancient past of the Fae. They had something to do with our origins, when we rose up from dryads before known history." I don't know the complete story. I suppose Marielle would have studied and remembered the details. "They're supposed to have died out, though."

Could these really be dragons? And why would Queen Maelys want to capture them? That would be unthinkable. They should be revered, not hunted.

Gundega tucks her little shovel back in the carrysack and rasps, "If it's the Queen, for sure she's up to no good. But we can't stand here like fools speculating all day. We need to get going."

The crows have settled back on their perches. I wish I could portal us away from there, but healers generally don't portal. Besides, that's Warrior training, and requires knowing exactly where we are, and where we're going.

Caden takes us down a narrow pathway near the cliff edge of the clearing. He half guides, half carries Gundega as we work our way down to the main trail. After that it's easier going, and we don't have to take so many rests. There's plenty of fresh water from streams, and we have a few travel cakes left from our provisions, along with the food we forage.

After two days, we arrive at the base of Cougar Mountain. Caden guides us to a ravine near where the trail opens out onto Queensdale Valley. We can overnight there, then skirt around the narrow edge of the valley nearest Dragon's End.

It's clear that we should go to Queensdale because that's where my duty lies. But there are so many unanswered questions.

CHAPTER 27

The small band of Rocky Shorelanders hides a sturdy wagon off the trail, deep enough into the forest so that Minason and his grandmother won't run into it. They take care not to be overheard by them either. The dragons have probably seen it, but it's of no interest to them. Chance assigns his hunters to spy in rotating shifts, avoiding the Human keepers, but coming and going for many days so the dragons will get used to their occasional sight and scent, and view them as harmless. Chance is patient, aware that this may be the only opportunity his small colony will ever get, to achieve a boon from the Queen of the Fae and be rewarded with the land they so desperately need.

He has brought his best trackers and hunters, ones that are not impetuous, and can be trusted to stay silent. After a week of watching, he decides on the dragon with the silver ruff. Fancy, they call him. He's a bit smaller, about the size of a brown bear when his wings are tucked, and doesn't seem as smart as Blaze, the larger one. Also, he sometimes shambles about on foot.

The dragons and their two Human companions get their water from a stream that feeds a pool near their cave. Fancy has taken a liking to the pool. He's fascinated by the shiny fish, sometimes hooking one with his claws. They're not big enough for a meal, but he's entertained by the game of sometimes swallowing one whole, and other times flipping the writhing fish back into the water to catch again.

After weeks of spying, the hunters are finally ready, and the net is ready. It was the sturdiest fishing net from the Rocky Shores. The fishers were reluctant to part with it, but Chance persuaded them with the promise of a rich reward, a spacious and fertile location for their new settlement across the river from First Bend.

It took them days to string it up. While they were hauling and carefully placing the net up in the tree, they suffered many interruptions, having to evade the attention of Minason and Baba as they go about their daily activities. Though not so much the dragons, who have been hunting and exploring far afield and don't return every day.

The corners of the net are loosely attached between the two sturdiest branches hanging over the edge of the pool, above a small outcropping where Fancy likes to watch his shiny fish. Minason and his Baba will be away for at least two days, foraging for mushrooms that don't grow on this part of Cougar Mountain. He orders two of his hunters to wait in the tree, the other four hiding behind trees and undergrowth until Fancy shows up.

The next morning, they get their chance. Fancy lights down near the cave and stretches out to nap in the sunlight. Thinking this might be the opportune moment, the eager hunters look to Chance for instructions, but he signals they should wait in place.

Fancy naps for hours, but then he stirs, stretches, and waddles over to the pool to play his fishing game. He watches the fish patiently, like a cat. The hunters wait with bated breath.

Finally, he leans over the edge of the water to snag his first fish of the day and Chance gives the signal. The two in the tree cast their net over the unsuspecting dragon. He rears and thrashes, his tail knocking one of the hunters into the pool. He snatches a corner of the net with his teeth to fling it off. But the four hunters waiting behind the tree rush in to stake down the edges so he can't move. He roars and flails, his powerful tail still whipping back and forth unhampered. The soaked hunter jumps on his tail and sits on it until they can contain it in the net.

His roaring is so loud that Chance has to risk his hands near the razor-sharp fangs. He gets one hunter to sit on the dragon's head and winds a leather strap around his snout until he can't open his mouth.

They truss him up in the netting, making sure his wings are tucked, and wind the net around him ever tighter so he can't thrash or shake himself free. They avoid the sharp tips of the spikes along his neck and back. He's heavier than they thought he'd be, his wings, metallic scales and massive bone structure making him weigh more than a bear of the same size. The Shorelanders struggle to lift him, and he almost flips himself away from them. But they manage to heave him onto the wagon and strap him down in preparation for the dangerous trek down the mountain.

Fancy stops struggling and lies still on the wagon, watching the triumphant but exhausted hunters out of one eye.

One of the hunters steps close to the dragon to admire their handiwork. He examines his spinning golden eyes. Fancy stares at him, and within moments the hunter is entranced, captivated by the glamour dragons have always employed to induce loyalty and servitude.

The hunter stands staring at Fancy as the others start pulling the great wagon with their priceless treasure. They yell at him to get moving. But he abruptly whips out his knife and leaps on the corner of the wagon nearest his head. He frantically starts to saw and hack at the sturdy netting and ropes, trying to free the dragon. The other hunters rush at him and pull him off. He struggles fiercely as they pull him away from the wagon until one of them hits him on the head with a rock, knocking him out.

"He was staring at the dragon's eyes," a hunter observes.

"Cover its head. Use a carrysack. Those eyes must have some kind of power. Don't anyone look at them again." The furious Chance goes to kick the downed hunter but restrains himself and gets back to his objective. He growls at his followers irritably, "Leave him. He's no use to us anymore. He'll either survive and make it back home, or not. Keep an eye out behind us on the trail. I don't want him following us."

It takes them several days of strenuous labor to haul the wagon with its heavy cargo down the mountain trail. Sometimes the slope of the trail is easy, but more often they have to push back from below to prevent it from careening down the steep segments. Then they have to shove from the other end and pull it up the rising slopes. Fancy appears to be sleeping the whole time.

They arrive at a clearing near the base of Cougar Mountain, where it opens onto Queensdale Valley. It's still going to be a long haul since they have to take the path around its edge. They can't cross the valley directly, lest Blaze fly over and spot her captured fellow dragon.

It's late, almost dusk. Chance calls a halt, directing his hunters to make an encampment for the night, and put their stewpot to cook for a warm meal and a good night's sleep before they embark on the final stretch to Queensdale.

The exhausted hunters are looking forward to an evening of relaxation. But without warning, six warrior Fae appear at the edge of the clearing. The motionless dragon is clearly visible to the newcomers, trussed up on the wagon under the trees farthest from the trail. They stand at alert but keep their swords sheathed and bows slung on their backs. The tallest of them looks around the encampment, then steps forward. "Who commands you? I would speak to them."

Chance strides toward them, trying to hide his consternation. These are the Queen's Guard, the same who ejected him from her throne room when he tried to negotiate with Queen Maelys after the young Marielle's unfortunate demise. He draws himself up, though he still has to look up at the tall Fae warrior. "We are on a special mission for Queen Maelys, and not to be interfered with."

The captain doesn't try to hide the contempt in his voice, nor his hand resting on the hilt of his sword. "I remember you,

Chance of the Rocky Shorelanders. I am Attican, Captain of the Queen's Guard. We know all about your mission, and also that you were banished to your own side of the peninsula after your gang of ruffians murdered our Queen-to-be. Release the dragon to us and you can go unharmed back to where you came from."

"I think not." Chance sweeps his arm around the clearing, where his five remaining hunters stand with crossbow bolts aimed at the Fae Guards. "We don't want to use these against you, but don't try to claim more authority than you have. Your Queen offers an excellent reward for anyone who brings her one of the dragons, and that includes us. You know that as well as I do, so don't try to steal it from us."

"We're the dedicated Guard to Queen Maelys, charged with bringing the dragon to her without delay." Attican removes his hand from the sword hilt. "It doesn't matter who actually captured it," he concedes. "We don't want to deprive you of your reward, but we Fae warriors have the ability to portal. We can transport the beast in moments over long distances. We can deliver it to her palace in two or three jumps, before that stew you're cooking is ready to eat."

Chance tells his hunters to stand down. "How many can you portal with you?" He too is eager to deliver the captive dragon to the Queen, confident he'll receive his reward of land across from First Bend. He's already relishing the thrill of announcing their new settlement to the Rocky Shorelanders. "I'm willing to let you do it if we all go."

He and Attican negotiate further. A portal will not convey more than six with this much cargo. They agree that he and two other Shorelanders, and three Fae Guards will portal to Queensdale palace with the dragon. The rest will portal after, everyone giving promises of good behavior.

Chance orders his hunters to cooperate with the Fae. He cautions them not to start any trouble, but to keep their crossbows at the ready just in case.

Fae and Humans together pull the wagon to the center of the clearing, amid much muttering and shoving, though they follow orders. Fancy shifts slightly in his netting, but remains quiescent. Captain Attican explains that he's going to cast an enchantment that will open a doorway to another location. Everyone must help push the wagon quickly through the portal, but only the designated six will pass through with the dragon. He indicates where everyone should stand.

They all wait, poised. The captain raises both hands and draws a complex pattern in the air, speaking buzzing words the Shorelanders can't make out. A large opening appears. Through it they see a field covered with volcanic ash. They quickly push the wagon through.

But the field vanishes as soon as the dragon passes into the portal. They are still in the same clearing near the base of Cougar Mountain. They stand and look at one another as the captain curses in frustration. One of the hunters snickers.

Attican directs everyone where to stand for another attempt. This time the portal is wider, and Dragon's End Mountain is visible in the background, trailing plumes of ruddy smoke. They ready themselves to push. He draws the enchantment and speaks the words.

But again, the portal vanishes as soon as the dragon enters it. The Queen's Guard confer with one another, to see if anyone knows a variation of the spell that will let the dragon through. But they have all had the same training, and there are no variations.

He confers with Chance again, and they agree to send only two from each party through the portal. But that doesn't work either.

"So, it looks like no portal for this dragon." Chance motions to his hunters to back off and keep their mouth shut. He wants to stay in the good graces of the Fae, but can't hide a trace of sarcasm. "I don't suppose you'll be willing to leave it to us, since we're the ones who captured this dragon. Those Human keepers called it Fancy, in case you were wondering."

"It should have worked." Attican is angry and frustrated, but keeps his composure. "We've been able to portal all sorts of creatures."

"We'll have to cooperate and bring it to her Royal Highness the slow way, as long as you Fae will help with the pushing. But we can be generous." Chance gestures to the stewpot simmering on the fire. "If we all share our travel cakes, there's enough stew to feed everyone. You're welcome to join us in the clearing for the night. Maybe we'll be good neighbors after all."

Attican is frustrated and embarrassed at his failed portals. But he concedes that the Guards have been searching for days and would appreciate a break from their trail rations.

They move the wagon back to the edge of the clearing and each group sets a rotation of two Fae and two Shorelanders to keep guard overnight, at opposite sides of the clearing to prevent fighting. They settle in wary detente, the two groups eyeing each other with suspicion, at opposite sides of the clearing as they make camp and prepare their meal. Fancy continues to lie quietly. Nobody knows if he's awake or sleeping.

CHAPTER 28

Caden is familiar with this part of Cougar Mountain. He explored it as a youth, and patrolled the area as a Ranger. I'm still not sure I can trust him, but my traitorous heart quivers each time I see him gazing at me, which is whenever we stop for even a moment. He usually holds Gundega by the hand to keep her steady, and I wish it was my hand in his. But no, I have to keep focused on my duty. On making it to Queensdale.

The trail is still surrounded by deep forest, but the slope is increasingly easy to manage. When we arrive at the base of Cougar Mountain, he leads us off the main path, down an almost invisible animal trail to a small ravine. We scramble down its side to a flattened area near the bottom where we'll camp for the night under the enormous firs, hidden against accidental encounters. The loamy forest smell is comforting after all that time in the dry air of the dwarves' tunnels.

Caden carefully scouts the ravine for danger. I don't watch his muscular back and arms as he clambers between the trees. I don't watch his long fingers as he crouches and builds a small fire at our campsite, head bent to the task, pushing his hair back over his shoulder. I don't watch him as his gentle and capable hands form a cooking bowl from birchbark, to warm water so we can soak the last of the travel cakes we scavenged from the tunnels. I don't watch his lips as he asks Gundega to set an Unnoticeable ward around our camp, forming words instead of kisses. I don't. I don't.

Also, I don't know what I'll do when I get to Queensdale. Gundega notices me frowning and interrupts my worrying. "When we get to Queensdale, we look for the Venerable Dame. She's the oldest Fae. She helped me when the Queen was trying to glamour me into submission. I don't remember exactly where she lives, but I'll try to find her for you. I'm sure she'll be able to help you."

I wonder if the Venerable Dame will remember Gundega, but it's better than anything I can think of, and I do my best to stay calm as we settle for the night.

The little cat has stayed with us, though she's not quite so little anymore. She snuggles up to Gundega, now her adopted companion. "Spark," she says, "she should have a name. She came to us in the fire, so we'll call her Spark."

"She's a young bobcat," Caden observes. "You can tell by the little tufts at the top of her ears. I doubt she'll want to stay with us for much…." He puts his hand up to signal listening, and we all hear a creaking noise. It's not very loud, but it continues for several minutes on the trail just above our ravine. Eventually it's recognizable as a large wagon being dragged slowly, the creaking of its wheels accompanied by hushed conversation. Whoever it is moves on, and we don't hear anything else.

We return to our preparations for the night, glad to be well hidden, but curious about the wagon on what's usually a footpath, or ridden on horseback. We're just finishing our sparse rations when we hear shouting and a commotion, then loud conversation we can't make out. Caden kicks out the fire and hushes us. We hold our breath as he stealthily climbs back up the side of the ravine to see what's going on. He's gone for what feels like a long time. I've just started up the narrow path to look for him, when I almost bump into him creeping silently down the same way.

"It's a small company of Raiders, together with the Queen's Guard who found us outside the tunnels. They're in a clearing a short way down the path. The Raiders have captured one of those dragons who landed on the cliff. It's the smaller one, the one with the silver ruff around its neck. They have it trussed up in a wagon, and bound its snout so it can't roar. And they've put a sack over its head."

This is horrifying news. "Oh no! That's so wrong. Dragons are held in highest esteem among the Fae, even though we thought they disappeared long ago. I could imagine them trying to invite the dragon to meet Queen Maelys, but to capture one like this? It's unthinkable."

"The Queen's Guard tried to portal it to Queensdale, but they couldn't get through with the dragon. Now they're cooperating, planning to camp for the night and continue at first dawn."

"We've got to do something. Dragons should be revered, not trussed up like animals. We've got to stop them. We've got to free the dragon." I almost shout, turning to head up the path, but just in time, I remember to keep my voice down.

Caden gently takes my shoulders and looks intently at me, his eyes warm and earnest. "Sislie, stop. There are only three of us, and they are many, and warriors. I can't imagine how we could do anything to set it free." His voice is low, coaxing. "We need to keep you safe. We've got to get you to Queensdale."

I shrug him off my shoulders, but he's right. I start pacing around our little camp, wracking my brain, but nothing.

Gundega is sitting near the remains of our fire, stirring in the birchbark bowl to soften the dried-out travel cakes. She mutters under her breath and looks up at me. "I wish I had thought to bring some of that sleeping powder. We might have found a way to sneak it into their food."

"Wait, wait." Caden jumps up and digs in his carrysack. He takes out a small pouch and a waxy envelope. He hands them to Gundega. "The Queen gave me this, to keep Sislie subdued. It's probably like the sleeping powder you had." When he sees my scowl, "I almost forgot I had it. And look, this other one, my mother gave it to me. It opens part of your mind. For clear seeing."

She opens the envelope and sniffs, then goes to stick her finger in for a taste. "Don't, Gundega. She said it's very strong. She gave me some before I started looking for Sislie. It gave me the vision of her dancing. And glowing." He looks at me with those eyes. "If it gave me visions, could it do the same for the Raiders and Guards?"

I take a sniff too. "I know some of these herbs. We would use them for serious pain, though not in this combination. It could work, but how do we get it to them?"

Caden leans toward me, eyes sparkling. "Sislie, you can *flicker*. How far can you *flicker*?" Once again, he's thought of another use for what's only been a dance move to me.

"I have the Magnification spell to make myself look big," Gundega jumps in. "Is there a tiny spell? To make you look small?"

"No, but I could disguise myself brown and green to look like a Dryad." I look at Caden. I may not be sure of him, but he's obviously very capable and has a good imagination. I decide to take the chance. "Caden, maybe we can do this. Let's go and look."

Caden empties the waxy envelope into the pouch from the Queen and hands it to me. We creep up the narrow path between the tall trees to the main trail, careful not to disturb any animals or step on dry twigs. Their encampment is just down the trail from our ravine. We see sentries on two sides of their clearing.

I cast an Unnoticeable glamour on both of us so their eyes will slide away from us if they hear us. We creep around the edge of the clearing. I almost shriek when one of the Fae sentries glances sharply in our direction, but we stand motionless in the dark and he turns back to his fellow sentry, who is complaining about having to collaborate with Raiders. As we steal past the bound dragon, it stirs briefly, but then is still. Finally, we arrive at a spot behind the trees nearest the campfire. Luck is with us. A Raider and a Queen's Guard are tending a stewpot. Apparently they're planning to share the meal.

I whisper in Caden's ear, "How can I get the powder to the stewpot? It's close enough to *flicker*, but someone will see me even if I'm Unnoticeable, and disguised as a Dryad."

He thinks for a moment, then a bright gleam lights up his eyes. "I'll provide a distraction. Wait until you see everyone turn and run toward the dragon, then *flicker* in."

"No, no." I grab his arm and can't hide the whispered panic in my voice. "They'll capture you."

His eyes are still sparkling. "Nothing like that. Look what I can make." He rummages around on the ground for a few minutes, coming up with a straight twig. He fletches it with some small feathers and sharpens it to a point with his hunting knife. It's a tiny arrow. "It won't do him any harm, but I'm going to shoot this at the dragon. That'll make him jerk and thrash around, and everyone will go running to the wagon."

Before he leaves to skulk around to the other side of the clearing, I refresh his Unnoticeable glamour so he won't attract the attention of the guards, especially the Fae. The dragon is lying in the wagon, glaring at his captors with one eye, where the hood has slipped sideways off his head. I can't see Caden from where I'm hiding near the campfire, but I'm ready. I look like a Dryad. Unnoticeable. I blend into the forest. I wait.

Without warning, the dragon twitches and starts to buck and thrash.

"What in the hells!" The Queen's Guard Captain rushes over to the wagon.

"Don't look at his eyes!"

"Make sure his ropes are tight." Everyone races to the dragon.

Now is my chance. It's a longer *flicker* than I'm used to, and I land a few steps from the stewpot. Heart slamming in my chest, I dash over with the pouch of powder. I empty it into the simmering stew, holding my breath so I don't inhale any of it. Just as I'm shaking the last grains into the pot, one of the Queen's Guards turns back toward the campfire. I almost faint as he frowns and takes a step in my direction.

Dryad. I'm a dryad. No different from the trees behind me. Unnoticeable. I'm frozen in fear, but I keep chanting to myself. *Dryad. Nothing to see here.* It's a small forever, but eventually his eyes slide away from me and he inspects the area of the campfire, then returns to the commotion around the wagon. I *flicker* back to the edge of the clearing, panting with fear, and then work my way back behind the trees.

The Raiders speculate among themselves, wondering what made the dragon thrash like that. "What was that about?"

"Did something bite it?"

"Maybe it's hungry."

The Queen's Guard do a thorough search around the wagon, but nobody spots the small makeshift arrow lying on the ground in the dark.

The Raiders and the Guard are all tired and cranky after their frustrating day, and hungry for something to eat other than trail rations. As soon as everyone settles down, the cooks distribute the stew among them, and to our great relief, the leader of the Raiders, a tall burly fellow with a bald head and gold chains around his neck, orders the cooks to bring bowls to the sentries on duty. They all hungrily gulp their stew as Caden steals his way back to me, grinning happily.

Without thinking, I grab him and kiss him, then jump back, embarrassed. He leans in for another kiss, but I push him away, blushing, and point to the sentries. We keep watch for a long time. At some point, we find ourselves holding hands. I'm not sure how that happened, but I like the feel of his muscular hand wrapped around mine.

In the clearing, they finish the rest of the stew with second helpings for almost everyone. Some of the Raiders start laying out their bedding, and others gather around for what looks like a game of dice. The Fae keep their distance, settling down at the farthest edge of the clearing from the Raiders. We wait some more. Still nothing. After a while we look at each other, disappointed that our best and only chance to save the dragon was wasted.

But just as we start to make our way back to the ravine, one of the Raiders calls out for his mother. He jumps up from his seat near the fire and runs into the woods howling and crying, "Mama, mama, where are you? I can't find you."

Another one yells and screams that the boat is about to capsize, and he takes off down the trail. The burly leader jumps up and shouts that the fire is leaping too high and turning into a conflagration. He runs to the stream, looking for water to fight the fire. The Raiders all start to cry, scream, run away, mill around, and fight with one another.

Last of all, the Fae Guards succumb, all at once seeing the forest turning into Dryads. They start to dance and weave among the trees with their eyes closed, enchanted.

Caden and I don't hesitate. We rush over to the wagon. Caden slashes the netting wrapped around the dragon, and the ropes securing it to the wagon. I take Gundega's cooking knife and gingerly remove the bindings on its snout. It seems to be unharmed, though I'm not able to feel into its body with my healing ability. Caden whistles tunelessly as he works his way around the wagon. The dragon waits, unmoving, and lets us do our work. When he's done, Caden lifts off the remains of the netting and ropes. We step back.

The dragon stands up on the wagon, snorts, and hops off, all turquoise and silver, glimmering in the light of the campfire. It looks down at me, golden eyes whirling. <<*FFFANSSSY*>> I feel, rather than hear, the word susurrate inside my head. Is that its name? His name? He gives his tail and ruff a shake and roars once at the pandemonium of Raiders and Guards. He crouches and springs, spreads his wings and launches into the evening sky without a backward glance.

I'm awestruck at this splendid being, his glistening wings scattering light like droplets around the clearing as he flies off. He is a tale out of legend, magnificent and powerful.

But no matter how reverential I feel, we don't have time to stand and stare in amazement. Caden takes my hand and we race back to our ravine, my feet barely touching the ground until we scuttle down the side of the ravine to where Gundega is waiting, little Spark curled up in her lap. She has gathered our rations and carrysacks, and filled the waterskins, anticipating a swift departure. We have no idea how long the effects of the powder will last, and we're not going to wait around to find out. I'm exhilarated, but scared the guards will come to their senses before we get away.

We return to the main trail and hustle down the path, Caden again supporting Gundega, though her limp is much better. He frequently monitors for anyone else in the area, and a few times we have to step off the path and hide behind trees or bushes to avoid night travelers. Each time Gundega refreshes our Unnoticeable glamour.

We don't sleep that night, tramping with hardly a pause until the morning light lends its soft color to the leaves of the forest.

The trail opens into a flat expanse covered in a thin gray layer of volcanic ash, with the pale green haze of spring valiantly pushing through. In the distance, we can see Queensdale Palace emerging from the early morning mist, with its lofty spires formed by trees coaxed and enticed over centuries into the shapes of halls, dwellings and towers. I've been there twice, for the Moon Festival ball, when I was younger and helped to serve refreshments to the dancers. I was going to perform there myself when Marielle was anointed. But that's not going to happen.

There are several grand tents on a wide field in front of the palace, with colorful banners proclaiming the Clans represented there. They're already gathering for the Grand Conclave? What if I'm too late? I try not to panic. I take a deep breath, ignoring the crawling feeling in my stomach. I steel my resolve and stride toward the main trail crossing the valley.

Caden catches up to me and gently takes my arm. He turns me back to the edge of the forest.

Gundega agrees, "It's safer this way. We don't want to be seen by the Queen's Guard." She shakes off his offer to help her walk, and limps off with her new staff, which he trimmed and whittled for her on the mountain.

We trudge along a narrow trail that skirts the short edge of the valley, just inside the treeline. Worn out after our sleepless night, we're still determined to get as far as we can during daylight. Caden has a free hand now that he's released from helping Gundega, and that hand keeps brushing against mine. After the third time, I take it. His hand is strong and warm, long fingers wrapping around mine. His smoldering eyes turn to me and make a promise I'm not sure I can accept. I walk on, trying not to cling, but reassured by his touch.

Toward mid-day we hear shouting on the main trail down the middle of the valley. We crouch behind a thicket to peer out at the commotion. It's the Queen's Guard from the night before, but I guffaw when I realize we don't have to worry about them noticing us.

They're jogging toward the palace, looking like a procession of clowns. One of the Guards trips into the Captain, who turns to chide him but instead spins around and falls backwards into a thicket of brambles at the edge of the trail. They stumble and argue, shoving each other off the path, but then fling their arms over each other's shoulders, and sing bawdy songs like drunken revelers. The Captain stops and tries to draw a portal in the air, cursing loudly when it fails. We snort and laugh out loud, even Gundega, covering our mouths so we don't make too much noise.

That night we finally sleep, exhausted, nestled under a sloping outcropping near the edge of the trail. Gundega places the Unnoticeable glamour over us and the rock.

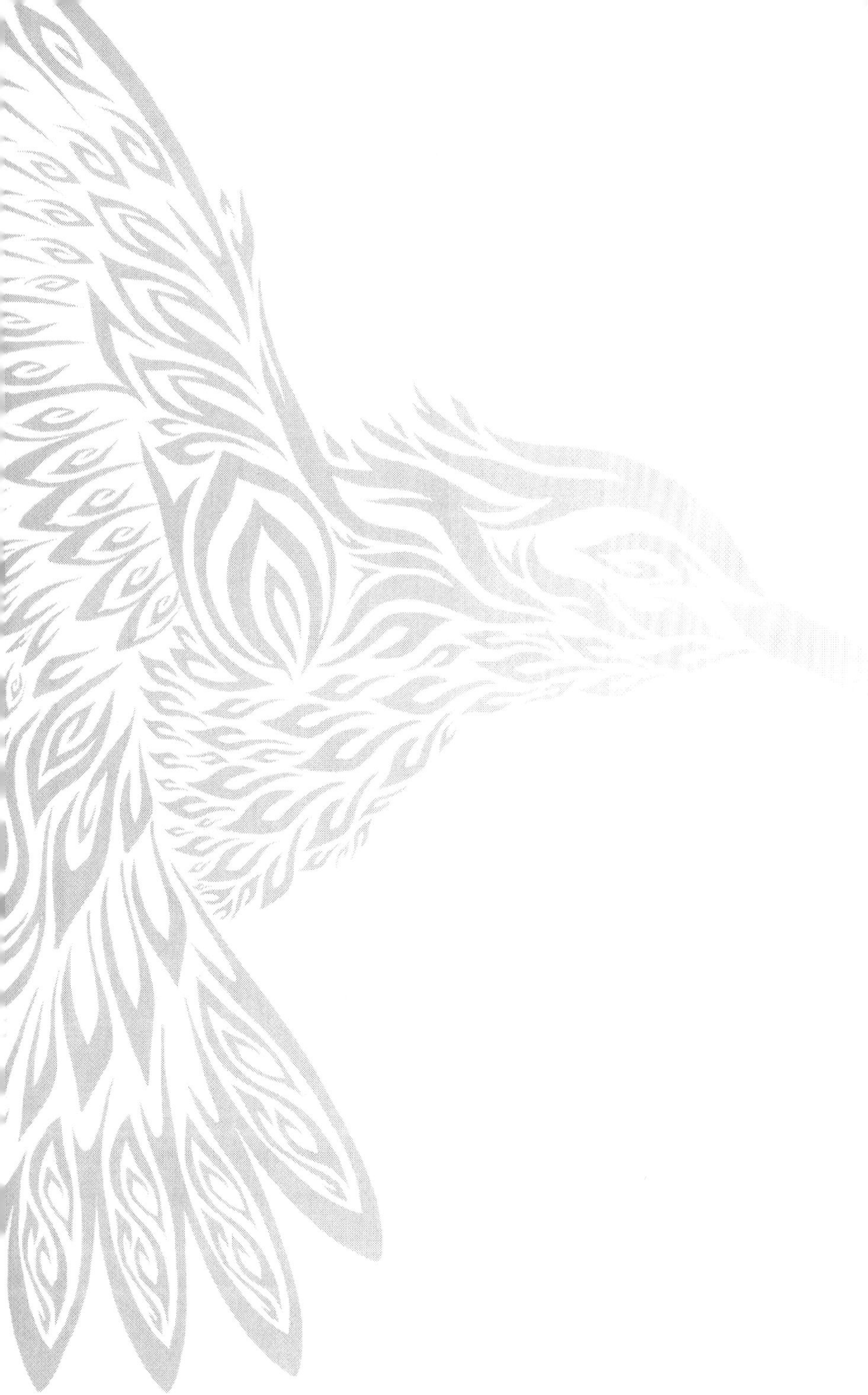

CHAPTER 29

The pale moon casts no shadow from behind its cloud as a black-cloaked figure slips through a narrow portal not far from their outcropping. He pauses, listening, then traces a Revealing spell on the trail that skirts Queensdale Valley. Edging forward, his footsteps are silent.

He stops, listens again. The only sounds are from the scurrying of night animals, occasionally punctuated by the squeal of an unlucky mouse as it becomes a hungry owl's meal. Nothing. He moves on.

The next time he pauses he can hear faint snoring from behind an outcropping near the edge of the trail. His soundless tread takes him around to the open side, where another Revealing spell shows him the three sleeping figures sheltered beneath.

He examines them, looking for the blonde curly hair he's been ordered to locate. But there's not enough light to distinguish between the three shapes, even with his keen night vision. He draws a long, thin dagger from a hidden sheath inside his cloak. He forms a tiny ball of light in his other hand and steps closer. The middle figure is his target. He takes a final step, crouching and raising the dagger to complete his task.

Just as he begins his thrust, there's a sudden hiss and a snarl, and a small bobcat leaps up and pounces on him. The dagger goes flying as he fights off the ferocious teeth and claws. He tries to grope for his other dagger, but the cat won't let go and the sleepers are roused. He's forced to flee, disappearing through a hastily drawn portal.

"What's going on?" Gundega rolls over and sits up.

Spark is yowling at the edge of the outcropping and Caden is on his feet, rushing out to see what's there, hunting knife in his hand.

I make a ball of light so we can see. There's nothing. But wait. A fleeting brightness blinks in the shadows by the trail as the moon comes out from behind a cloud. It almost looks like it could be a portal.

Caden returns to our outcropping. He shakes his head. "There's nobody out there. No animals, either. I can't figure out why Spark made such a commotion. She wouldn't do it for no reason."

"Must have been a cougar that got too close," Gundega offers.

"But there's nothing out there. I'd be able to sense it if there was."

"I thought I saw something on the trail." I hesitate to say anything, because I might have been imagining it. "It could have been a portal, but it's hard to tell. It was only a glimpse."

"There's no point in standing around guessing." Gundega starts to gather her belongings. "There'll be no sleep after this, and the sun will be up soon. We might as well get moving."

She's right. I could use a few more hours of sleep, but I'm too uneasy. I grab my cloak and carrysack and make for the trail, but Spark is meowing, nosing and pawing at something in the deepest recess of the stony outcropping. I bring my ball of light over to her. Something is glinting back there. I can't see what it is, so I crawl under the sloping roof and look closer.

What's that doing here? I reach in and pull out a long thin dagger with an obsidian handle. Suddenly my mouth is dry and my heart is slamming in my chest. I bang my head on the roof as I back out to the edge of our shelter, gingerly holding its handle between my fingers.

"Caden, look." My voice is shaking.

He takes the dagger in his hand and examines it closely. It's shiny and clean, not something lost or discarded long ago. "I saw one of these during my Ranger training." He looks at me with grim eyes. "It's a warrior's blade."

I'm still shaking as we make our way down the trail. A Fae warrior? A killer? I'm more scared than I've ever been, and more confused than I was in Gundega's cottage. Caden assures me he'll keep his sensing wide open for anyone nearby and Gundega keeps the Unnoticeable spell on us the whole day.

Eventually, I fall into the rhythm of walking. We still have to go slowly because of Gundega, but that probably helps because the forest and the fine day conspire to calm me down. And so does Caden, who holds my hand most of the time.

That night he makes us a shelter of fallen branches. We decide to sleep in shifts. He takes the first shift, and Gundega offers to take the second. I'll take the last one.

Nobody wakes me for sentry duty, but it's quiet when I wake up to the pink tracings of early dawn. There's an arm draped over me. It feels nice, but I gently slide it off so I can go to relieve myself behind the bushes. When I come back, Caden is standing outside our shelter, Gundega snoring inside.

He takes a step toward me and it's the easiest thing in the world to lean into his arms. All of my worries slide off me as I melt into the smoldering gaze of his violet eyes. I surrender to the warmth that rises from under my belly, my lips questing for his. We merge into each other, taking the other's face in our hands and tasting hungry lips. His voice murmurs, "Sislie" as his strong Ranger's arms lift and carry me to a small hollow on the other side of the trail. He spreads his cloak on a bed of moss and we sink down onto the softness.

He traces the side of my brow, cheek and jawline with his finger, then marks those same places with his lips, taking a nibble of my earlobe on the way. He strokes my shoulders, but then pushes me to arm's length, gazing a question into my eyes while his fingers play with the cord that holds the front of my shift.

My lips smile yes as I undo the fastenings of his leather jerkin. It perfectly enfolds his muscular chest, simple loops holding it in place until it slips from his shoulders. I reach under his shirt and slide it up and over his head, feeling his back muscles with my hands as my mouth traces the contours of his throat.

My nipples thrill and harden as he reaches inside my camisole, then draws it up over my head. His lips and tongue nibble and explore down my neck, his playful fingers investigating the curves of my body. When his feathery touch discovers and explores my wing nubs, I gasp and arch my back, pressing toward him. My senses are wide open, open to him, ready.

But my senses are also open to everything—the forest, the animals, the land surrounding us. And seekers. With a shock of recognition, I feel the Clan seekers questing for me. Reality intrudes, together with my duty, and this destiny I never wanted. I gasp and push him away, my dismayed eyes watching his passion turn to shock and disappointment. "No. Caden, I can't. I'm sorry. I'm promised."

"What? You re promised to another? You could have told me." Now it's bewilderment and anger in his eyes.

"No, no, it's not that, I'm promised to the Land. I'm supposed to be anointed at the Grand Conclave. To be the next Fae Queen." The words tumble over each other. "Oh Caden, we have to go. You saw me dancing. That was the real me. My cousin Marielle was going .... She was killed by Raiders...."

"Marielle. I heard about her. You're her cousin. You're the new Fae Queen Designate." The hurt in his voice merges with my dismay and plummets to the bottom of my heart like a heavy stone.

His eyes harden, and he doesn't try to hide the bitterness in his voice. "You're unattainable. Forbidden. The Queen of the

Fae can't mate with a halfbreed like me." He grabs his shirt and jerkin and jumps to his feet, stomping off into the trees.

Gundega's croaky voice intrudes as I'm hastily getting back into my clothes. "We need to get moving."

I grab his cloak and carry it back to our shelter with a heavy heart. Once again, what I want is overshadowed by duty and disappointment.

We skirt the edge of the valley for two more days, staying alert for danger, sleeping in shifts. We walk single file, Gundega between us. Caden and I don't look at each other. I revisit what happened between us, over and over again. My body's restless and agitated. I keep thinking he could love a dancer, if only I could be that dancer. I could love him. It wouldn't be forbidden.

We forage for mushrooms and nuts, and there are a few early shoots. Occasionally we find a few dried berries remaining on the bush from last summer. We avoid the young Fae exploring the woods, already gathering fuel for the giant bonfires that will light the evenings during the Grand Conclave.

Several times I try to talk to him, to explain. But he just turns away.

CHAPTER 30

The Captain of the Guard flinches at her shriek. Tiny will-o'-the-wisps burst out of chandelier formation, bolting to cower in the corners and behind the tapestries of the Queen's drawing room. The ladies-in-waiting all fall to their knees, hiding their faces and surreptitiously covering their ears.

"You let it get away! You had it and you let it escape!" Queen Maelys is apoplectic, eyes bulging, skeletal face contorted in fury, lipless mouth spitting in rage, Youthfulness glamour disintegrated. "You let it go!"

"I beg your mercy, Majesty. There's no excuse. An unknown malady came over all of us, including the Humans. In the morning, the dragon was gone and the net restraining it cut to pieces."

"Idiots! You were drugged."

"That's not poss... but we did share food with the Humans."

"Of course it's possible, you witless fool." She pauses a moment, regaining her composure, and refreshing her Youthfulness glamour. "It could also have been a Fae, one of your Guards, or you're not the only ones who know how to portal.

Who else was on that mountain? Never mind, just find that dragon. Go. And don't come back until you bring it to me."

Kairon rushes in as she's giving the order, drawn by the commotion. "Gracious Majesty, the Grand Conclave is fast approaching and we still haven't located Sislie. Surely that must be the priority. Captain Attican can send a squad of his best Guards to continue searching for the birds, though they couldn't really be dragons." He continues at her brief nod, relieved that contradicting her directly didn't incite another tirade. "I'll accompany the Captain to help find her."

"Majesty, we also encountered the Queen Designate on Cougar Mountain," the shame-faced Attican confesses. "We were about to escort her to Queensdale when the dragons appeared. We pursued of them instead, as you ordered. She's travelling with a young Ranger and that old Gundega. I expect they're headed in this direction."

"You lost them both," the Queen is muttering now, exhausted by her tirade. "You couldn't find them all winter and when you finally did, you imbeciles lost them both." She flaps her hand at the Royal Consort. "Find them. No, Kairon, you must stay here. Take me to my chambers. I'm tired."

Kairon gestures to a servant to have the palanquin brought for her Gracious Majesty.

As though echoing the Queen's fury, Dragon's End Mountain shudders again, spewing another cloud of smoke and ash. A new fissure splits the cave where Minason sheltered the scrawny birds. Chunky a-a lava starts to clink and crawl out onto the plateau, obscured for now by the thick smoke. Two young dragons speed toward Dragon's End, relentlessly circling the smoky peak when they get there. Their fascination with the crevasse where they were born has been transformed into urgent hunger.

Farther down, on the opposite side of the mountain, Minason's uncle Brom, the headman, orders the Asmung tribe to leave their village. Gathering their belongings and loading them onto carts and donkeys, they hasten down the mountain, finally abandoning the toxic stream that's been laying waste to their tribe for the last hundred years.

CHAPTER 31

The next afternoon the mountain roars again, and the ground shudders. We rush out of the trees to find out what's happening, but the top of Dragon's end Mountain is eclipsed by a thick cloud of smoke, so we can't see much. We hurry on our way, soon followed by an ashy cloud that settles over the valley as fine grey dust that stings if we touch it, and has an acrid smell.

By the time we arrive at the outskirts of the palace grounds, the smoky daylight is fading. We're out of food, hungry, tired and cranky. Caden has hardly spoken a word to me since that morning.

I wonder out loud where exactly we should go. Gundega reminds us. "We should find the Venerable Dame. She'll help us decide what to do."

"Who's that?" Caden asks.

"I met her when Queen Maelys first summoned me. She helped me. Her chalet is somewhere near here."

A figure emerges from behind a narrow spire. She's a tall Fae, soft and glowing. Her wings are unfurled and hang like a shimmering cape, as does her long silver hair. Her eyes are deep and luminous, the violet almost silver. She looks ancient beyond years, her skin soft, loosened by her many decades. She beckons to us with one hand, turns, and seems to float away toward a secluded edge of the palace grounds. Gundega follows without hesitation. Caden and I exchange a curious glance, then go after her.

She leads us to a hidden doorway and welcomes us into a parlor draped with ancient glowing tapestries. One of them depicts amazing creatures—giants and dragons, enormous and beautiful, fire exploding out of a mountain, battles, fantastic birds and animals. A servant is setting out tea from a tulip shaped teapot into delicate porcelain cups. We hungrily eye the tiny cakes, fruit, and nuts heaped on a gracefully coaxed table at the center of the room.

"Venerable Dame..." Gundega awkwardly starts to kneel, but the ancient Fae takes her hand and raises her to her feet.

"I remember you, Gundega. Sit and rest," she says, gesturing to all of us. "Take some refreshment and then I'll hear your tale." She takes in Caden with her eyes and gives me a long look. "I am Ylva, the oldest of the Fae. Most trust me, even the Queen, though less now than long ago when we were close friends."

We sit down uneasily on the elegant chairs, thankful for their comfortable brocade cushions, but conscious of how dirty and unkempt we are, with our travel-stained clothes and ashy skin and hair. I gobble down a spiced raspberry cake, hardly noticing the delicious burst of flavor in my mouth. But a crunchy bite of nut bread suddenly tastes like home. A memory glimpses my mother serving me a slice of that same nut bread on one of her favorite yellow tea plates, and my eyes brim with tears.

The Venerable Dame sits at ease on her silken brocade settee, unfurled wings softly wrapped around her like a diaphanous cloak. She watches us eat with her soft eyes.

Our hunger subsided, all three of us lean forward, full of the many things we want to ask. The questions are swirling around in my brain faster than the spinning lights of my most intricate choreography. She holds up her hand to stay the questions and turns to me. “Now, what of you, young Queen-to-be? We were all horrified at the murder of your cousin Marielle. You are the next in line from the Hummingbird Clan?”

“Not just next, but the only one of suitable age in the Clan, Venerable Dame.” My voice chokes as I try to talk through the tears threatening to burst through. I see Caden from the corner of my eye, crossing his arms and scowling. “Marielle was the regal one. I never wanted this. I’m not ready, and it’s almost time for the Grand Conclave.”

She smiles at me. “I can see that you are clever and courageous, qualities just as important for a Queen as scholarship and wisdom. I have every confidence you will make a fine queen. But first we have to get you there.” As she speaks her whole being glows, and she reaches to take my hand. I take a deep breath, her voice and touch giving me strength.

Gundega leans forward on the edge of her chair and interrupts, “Why is it spring already? We weren’t in the tunnels more than a couple of tendays.”

The Venerable Dame turns to her and says, “You were in the dwarf tunnels? They hold many secrets, one of them is the swiftening of time.”

“But how?” we all ask, almost with one voice.

"The dwarves had their own unique magic, different from Fae and Elves. they were in possession of some deep mysteries. Their knowledge disappeared when they vanished from the Land long ago. It's an intriguing question, but for another time."

She turns back to Gundega. "I remember when you disappeared as a child. You might have become one of the great coaxers of the Lynx Clan. Gundega. Is that the name the Asmung gave you?"

"I believe so, Venerable Dame. It's the only name I know."

"Would you like to know your Fae name?"

Gundega's eyes brighten, eager and hopeful for a moment, but then her face wilts in sorrow. "No, it's just as well I don't. They wouldn't want me back, broken as I am. There's no point wanting what can never be."

"Perhaps it's just as well. There is another broken Fae in court, whom you will no doubt meet. Ned. He was injured by Raiders at the same age, and also looks like an aged Human. But don't trust him. He's a spy for Queen Maelys." Her look becomes stern. "She also groomed you to be her agent. Tell me why you kidnapped the designated Fae Queen-to-be."

"Venerable Dame, it was a despicable thing to do. I know that now." Gundega squirms and shifts around in her chair, eyes averted. "Queen Maelys rewarded me for doing errands from time to time, and taught me some spells. After a few visits, I grew to believe she could be trusted."

I've never seen the gruff Gundega cry. She covers her face with her hands, talking through her tears. "She persuaded me that Sislie was in danger from the Raiders. I believed I was keeping her from harm. She gave me this cloak, to help me capture her. It can take on different appearances, or become a sack with magical properties." She looks up at me, angry and remorseful. "I wish I had never met that wicked hag."

We sit in silence for a long moment. "It's unfortunate, but it's done and we can't change that." Ylva turns her soft eyes to Caden. "There is Fae blood in you too, young friend. Is it your mother or father?"

"It's my father, Madam, though I've never known him."

She notices the rancor in his voice. "The Fae are not always able to acknowledge their progeny, especially those at court, and usually for reasons of safety." She holds her hand up to stop his retort. "You may never have met him in person, but he has probably helped you in other ways. Interesting and useful gifts, perhaps, or help and guidance from unexpected quarters."

He looks perplexed at this. "Yes, actually. My mother would sometimes find gifts on our verandah, and from time to time I'd see someone in the forest near our homestead, but she explained it away as dryads."

"Your mother is from foreign lands?"

"No, she grew up in First Bend. But my grandfather came from over the sea. He was a trader, and married my grandmother, who came from Raven's Harbor."

"Ah yes, that explains the charming curve of your eyes and your honey complexion. What Fae talents do you have?"

Caden shuffles uneasily, unused to anyone recognizing his Fae qualities, much less taking them for granted. "I can see things that others can't, through glamours. I can sense the forest and who is there, animals or Human, also Fae, unless they wear the Unnoticeable glamour. Then I only see through it if they're close to me. I can light kindling without using a flint."

I startle, realizing I can do that too. The steel and flint at Gundega's cottage always put my teeth on edge.

Caden continues, "My arrows shoot straight, though I think that's helped by my bow, which my mother gave me when I became a Ranger. I'm told it's elven-crafted."

"Let me see. May I touch it?" He releases it to her without hesitation. She takes it gently in her hands and peers at the flat surface of the bow. She sketches a Magnification spell over it, and amber colored runes rise up from the pale wood. Caden gasps to see the characters, different from the single elven glyph at its tip.

"What does it say?"

"Whose heart is true, their aim is true." She hands the bow back to him. "It's most surely a gift from your father." She ignores his look of surprise. "What else can you tell me?"

The Venerable Dame notices me squirming and reaches out her hand, inviting me to sit next to her on the settee.

"I heard Sislie had gone missing. At first I thought it would be a fine adventure, but then I saw her in a vision. She was dancing, surrounded by light. I knew I had to save her." He glances at me but continues. "The Fae Queen's entourage stopped me as I was leaving the village. I didn't want her reward, but a courtier with her used the Ranger's hand language to warn me."

"Ah yes, that would be Lord Kairon. He's a good friend to the Rangers, and to the Queendom. He is the Queen's consort, but truly dedicated to the Land. She's gotten much worse in recent years, surrounded by corrupt and mendacious sycophants. He does his best to reduce the harm they cause."

"What's wrong with her?" I ask.

Caden and Gundega start talking at the same time. "Is that why she looked so mean under the Youthfulness glamour?"

"She was so persuasive, I didn't realize she was evil."

The Venerable Dame holds up her hand to stop us from babbling, "I know you have many questions, and I'll try to answer what I can. But there are things you need to know before you can go any further. Especially you, Sislie, because it had a direct bearing on the job ahead of you."

Her soft voice takes on a sonorous, chanting quality and we settle back to listen. "In the time before remembering, many of the inhabitants of the Land were gods. They were powerful, intelligent, and beautiful. But not wise. Or kind. They constantly warred with one another, and cared little for the giants who lived here, nor for the elves and dwarves. Not even the naiads, dryads and merfolk, new beings they themselves had created.

"They coexisted in a precarious truce with dragons, who were not of their creation but flew in from afar to eat the lava that erupted from the craters of Dragon's Peak."

"You mean Dragon's End?" I didn't mean to interrupt, but isn't that the name?

She glances at me and continues in her sonorous voice. "The mountain you know as Dragon's End was then an active volcano. It was much higher in those days and had an enormous crater at its peak. It often disgorged a kind of lava that was not liquid, but moved very slowly and made a crunching noise as it crackled out of the mountain. The dragons loved this a-a lava. They came to chew on it when they wanted to renew their fires.

"Meanwhile, the gods, powerful but reckless, battled continuously. They killed off all the giants, and ultimately almost killed each other off. Then they tried to enslave the dragons, who, of course, couldn't be made subservient to anyone. That war went on for centuries.

"Finally, exhausted by the warring and depleted in number, the gods tried to negotiate a truce. But the dragons were still furious at their attempts to enslave them and refused the truce. They captured all the children of the gods and flew them to the middle of the sea, where they cast them into the deeps.

"The oldest and most powerful god was enraged. In a fit of revenge, he lured the dragons to the mountain peak, where he ensorcelled them to gorge on the a-a lava until they were so glutted, they all fell asleep. He then deepened the crater to the very center of the mountain and hurled them all down into it. The lava closed in over them and even though they were lovers of fire, it was too much for them. The crater collapsed as they died, leaving a flattened mountain top.

"This was a catastrophe, but not just for the dragons. Because as they died, their hatred and fury released a powerful venom that poisoned the mountain and threatened to spread throughout the Land.

"After that, the gods persisted in their love of fighting, and, having killed all their foes, they eventually destroyed one another, until there was only one god still living. TAN. When she realized the enormity of what her fellows had caused, her heart filled with remorse. By then, the poison released by the dying dragons was defiling the Land and would ultimately destroy all its inhabitants.

"TAN wanted to make reparation for all the evil done by her fellow gods. She gathered an essence from the volcano, another from the sea, the air, the forest and the land, and molded them by starlight into a small vessel. She filled it with her tears of compassion for the Land, and used this to heal the poison. But it took all of her strength."

I'm leaning forward, completely entranced by her narrative. I would have paid more attention to my history lessons if this story had been part of the instruction.

"By this time, the Fae had been populating the Land. You know, of course, we Fae have always revered dragons. It was they that caused us to arise from the dryads. They gave us sentience, wings, and the ability to do enchantments.

"The first Queen of the Fae loved TAN greatly. She carried her to a deep grotto at the foot of Dragon's End Mountain, that was known to have healing powers. As the god lay dying in her arms, the Queen loved her so much that she sacrificed all of her heart fire trying to save her life, and died with her."

The Venerable Dame turns toward me. "Sislie, next is the part that pertains to you." She gazes at me intently, then at Caden and Gundega, listening in rapt attention. "It's a secret known to only a few, and I must know if you trust your companions to keep it. Otherwise, they'll have to leave the room while I tell you the rest."

I may not feel prepared to be Queen, but it doesn't take me any time at all to know I can trust my friends. "Venerable Dame, we've survived a forest fire, we've saved each other's lives, we've lived in tunnels and caves, traveled down a mountain, and rescued a dragon. How could I not trust them?"

"The god didn't truly die," she continues, acknowledging my friends. "With her last trace of will and intention, she merged her essence with the Queen and they became one. They submerged down to the bottom of the pool and entered a deep sleep. The Fae set guardians at the grotto so it would remain undisturbed. They developed the enchantment of Unnoticeability so the grotto and the castle the gods had built around it would be obscured.

"As she slept, TAN was slowly restored by the healing waters. After three hundred years, she returned with the vessel, containing an elixir infused with her essence. She bestowed this on a newly anointed Queen, so that she could in turn heal the land. Ever since then, she returns on the equinox of spring every three hundred years. That's why the Queen's reign is exactly three hundred years. The elixir gives her a longer life than most Fae and also guarantees the stability of the Queendom. When the three hundred years have passed, the old Queen guides the newly anointed Queen to TAN's grotto.

"It's commonly believed among the Fae that the old Queen relinquishes her rule and becomes one of the priestesses who guard the grotto. But what really happens is that the old Queen gives herself to the god, just as the first Queen did. She enters the pool of her own free will, to merge her essence and her body with the god TAN. She surrenders the vessel made from air, earth, fire, wood, water, and starlight, to the newly anointed Queen, who drinks its elixir and thus gains the power to heal the Land. If the Land is healthy, those who dwell on it will also be healthy."

I hear her words, but I can't take it in. I'm stupefied, aghast. Is this my duty? My fate? I knew I never wanted to be Queen, but this? To give my life? Did Marielle know about this? I push back into the settee, shuddering, but what I'd really like to do is run out of here, run away back to my willow glade and dance and dance and make it all go away.

The Venerable Dame sees my consternation. "Sislie, listen. It's three hundred years. It's a longer life than you would have otherwise. You'll have a long and wise reign, I can tell. You will be ready when the time comes. Trust this."

The Queen is the actual healer of the Land. It's not just symbolic. More questions pile up, and I have to hold back from spilling them out.

But the Venerable Dame gestures me to listen, and continues.

CHAPTER 32

"The land is healed, but this doesn't last forever. After about two hundred years, the healing essence is mostly used up and the poisons will again leech into the water and soil. Fortunately, this is not the water that flows to Queensdale or most of the Human towns, because our water comes from Raven's Peak. But the Asmung people, who live on the other side of Dragon's End Mountain, have been severely affected.

"The Asmung were always very peaceable, ruled by the Grandmothers. They traded pottery, leather craft, basket weaving, and rare mushrooms with both Human and Fae. They were a proud people, taciturn, honest, and good humored. But when the poison started to contaminate their water, it blighted the community. Many of the elders and children got sick and died, including the Grandmothers.

"Without their wisdom and calming good sense, the men of the tribe reverted to solving their problems by fighting among themselves. They then wrested leadership from the Grandmothers. They became more violent, even hitting the women and children. At the same time, they were losing their fertility.

Mothers were bearing fewer children, and they were increasingly unhealthy and underdeveloped.

"The Fae normally leave Humans and others to their own devices, but in this case we realized what was causing the trouble, and knew it would be decades before the new Queen of the Fae would come to heal the land. So, we decided to try to intervene.

"It was your mother and father," she continues, looking at me, "who went to help them. They even rode in on ceremonial cougars to impress them with the gravity of the situation. They explained about the toxins and where they were coming from, and offered to help the Asmung tribe move to a different mountain, or down to the valley on the other side, where there would be a fresh source of water. But the Asmung headmen scorned this advice, just as they had been ignoring the advice of the Humans from Caden's First Bend, claiming they just wanted to steal their land and resources.

"The traders had also tried to persuade them because their craft had deteriorated so much that it was no longer suitable for trade. But to no avail. Consequently, frustrated that nobody wanted their wares, they started to cheat and steal, and now nobody trusts them.

"The Fae would periodically visit and tried to help and heal them, but were not successful, and the toxins grow more powerful every year. Knowing the Fae were healers, one headman decided they should have their own Fae, and that was why they kidnapped Mina, and later you, Gundega. They believed they could raise you as their own and that you would heal them. Were you aware that Mina gave birth to a son?"

"Yes, she died giving birth to him. That's why I ran away."

"They named him Minason. He's grown into a fine young man in spite of the poisons and his dreadful upbringing. I've been to visit the few Grandmothers remaining, including Minason's Baba, and try to help the women as best I can, but the damage is done. I hope you and the elixir will be able to help them before it's too late."

The Venerable Dame stands up and beckons us to one of the tapestries in her drawing room, full of glimmering colors. "This is one of the oldest tapestries. It's different from the others. It shows not the past but possible futures."

She sketches a long and complicated Revealing enchantment in the air. At first nothing happens, but then the glimmer grows dull, as though veiled with a misty curtain. Dragon's End Mountain's distinctive contour becomes visible behind the veil, smoky remnants of the recent eruption idly coiling skyward.

As we watch, we can see deep into the mountain itself, into its churning bowel, where a dark and ruddy tumor leaks its noxious effluent, gradually seeping upwards to the surface. I recoil in horror and disgust. I want to shout out that someone needs to stop this, but I can't keep my eyes from the tapestry.

The motion speeds up and now we can see what's happening on the surface of the mountain. The remaining Asmung sicken and die. But the oozing doesn't stop there. It flows outward to the adjoining valleys and mountains, and time speeds up even more.

The mountain erupts again and again, spewing ever more venomous fumes over the land. The Humans and Fae are all poisoned, and the forests wither and burn, spreading their toxic flames to Queensdale, First Bend and beyond. Finally, the earth gives a horrendous shake and Queensdale valley, the center of the Land, splits into a colossal fissure, consuming the charred remains of the forest and Queensdale itself. The three mountains surrounding it sag as we watch, and slide and topple into the crevasse. Eventually, the cataclysm settles down, revealing a dead land of rubble and reddish smoke. No living thing survives.

Slowly, the misty veil dissipates, and the tapestry takes on its previous luminescence. I'm sickened and horrified. Caden and Gundega are both stunned, and stand unmoving. The Venerable Dame is back in her chair, tears flowing down the soft parchment of her cheeks. She asks us to return to our seats. We sit in silence for a long time, unable to take in the abomination we have just witnessed.

The Venerable Ylva takes a silken handkerchief from a pocket and slowly wipes her wet eyes and cheeks. She addresses me directly "And that is why, Sislie, your mission is so crucial. You already know it's not just a ceremonial position. But it's not just about the governance of the Land either. Nor just the healing of the Asmung, though they are the unfortunate first victims of the poison.

"Queen Maelys has abandoned her responsibilities to help and heal them, or the other Humans or Fae either. She has forgotten that the Queen is first and foremost the healer of the land. She even appears to be standing in the way of your anointing. If you fail to receive the elixir, nothing can stop the spread of the poison. The Land will be destroyed."

Her words pierce my soul. My heart is in anguish from the knowledge I've just been given. I now understand what I have to do, and why. I didn't choose this destiny, but it's mine. I finally accept it. What I want no longer matters. It's not just ceremonies, or governance, or prestige for the Hummingbird Clan.

I always thought healing the land was a symbolic thing. It's not. It's real, and very specific. So much more than being an ordinary healer. I just hope the weight of responsibility won't crush me. Sacrificing my dancing isn't so terrible in light of this.

I ask, my voice shaking, "What am I supposed to...?"

Caden jumps up from his settee and almost upends the dainty table in front of him. "We have to keep you safe. I have to keep you safe."

"Yes, we must." The Venerable Dame makes a calming gesture to Caden. "We'll take you to a haven where you can stay until the Grand Conclave. I will instruct you there as best I can. I have never been Queen, but Maelys was my friend when we were young, and she shared much of her knowledge with me. So I know most of what you need to learn.

"Queen Maelys is increasingly selfish, forgetful, and even cruel. You'll be safer away from her. She has been making poor decisions and is too much under the influence of Jarin and his coterie of greedy and duplicitous courtiers. Thankfully, we have a cadre of loyal allies in the court who work to keep things running and undo the harm she does.

"When the time comes, Lord Kairon will escort you directly to the Grand Conclave. He is the Royal Consort, but his first loyalty is to the Land, and to the Fae. He works hard to assuage the damage Maelys has done. Many of the Queen's Guard are loyal to him, some at court, and a good few servants and handmaidens, including Liana, who serves the Queen. They do their best to hold the palace safe until the new Queen is anointed.

"The Grand Conclave will last a fiveday. There are wonderful festivities, then ceremonies of dedication and promises for you to speak to each of the Clans, the Fae as a whole, the Humans, the elementals and the land itself. The Guardians of the grotto have a special ceremony near the end, which will ordain you as the true Queen."

She gracefully rises and leaves the drawing room to call her handmaiden. When she walks, it looks more like floating. I know that walk, and briefly wonder if she used to be a dancer.

After a few minutes, she returns with a handmaiden almost as old as she is. "You're all exhausted. Elena will show you to sleeping quarters, where you can spend the night. In the morning, she'll take you to the lodge and bring you food for the next few days. I will come to you whenever I can. The other Fae usually don't interfere with me or question what I do. But the Queen's Guards have been more meddlesome lately, and her spies are everywhere, so we may not be able to get to you every day."

I'm overwhelmed by the information I've received. I don't even remember the servant showing me to a bed, though in the morning I'm less exhausted. Elena takes us to the larder, fills our water skins for us, and gives us dried fruit, nuts, bread, and more travel cakes to tide us over in case it takes her a while to come to us.

The terrible knowledge of the destruction of the land grips me in its jaws like a hungry dragon. I'm still dazed from this new understanding of my role as Queen, and ashamed that I've been stubborn and self-indulgent. I'd really like to take a few days to think and rest and get used to accepting my new task. But mostly sleep. I'm standing lost in thought when I realize Caden is standing really close, talking to me.

"Sislie, I'm sorry for getting so mad. I didn't realize." He drops down on one knee and looks up at me with a resolute look on his face. "Sislie, Your Grace, I am at your service. I am forever at your service. Maybe I can't love you, but I can help you. And I will, in whatever way I can." When I don't say anything, he gets up and looks at me intensely. "Sislie, are you ok?"

I'm still tired, and so overwhelmed that my insides are quivering. I can't even appreciate his promise, much less his eyes. But I lean into his sturdy chest and let myself rest for a moment, closing my eyes and welcoming the comfort there.

The Venerable Dame comes to hurry us on. "You'll be staying in what was once a hunting lodge. It's up and around behind Queensdale Palace, in an area not much used. It is solidly built and safe from the elements. There are no predators in that area, so you won't have to worry about safety. I'll do my best to come up tomorrow at dawn, and we can start your lessons."

A loud hail from the front of her house interrupts her, "Venerable Dame, it's Attican, Captain of the Queen's Guard. We need to warn you of possible danger."

CHAPTER 33

Minason is drawing a picture of his Baba as she sits cross-legged in the shade of an oak tree, weaving a basket. He's still musing about where Fancy disappeared to for those few days. The young dragon sent him vague pictures a couple of times, of a large wagon and a beautiful young Fae, but Minason could never decipher what he was trying to tell. Maybe Blaze can get more information from him.

Blaze and Fancy interrupt his thought as they land in a flurry and playfully spurt sparks of flame around the clearing. "Stop it." Minason jumps up and runs toward the dragons, flapping his arms and scolding. "You mustn't do that. Last time you ruined our drying rack and nearly burned up Baba's favorite blanket. And you don't want to start another forest fire."

The dragons pretend to ignore him. They tussle with each other in the middle of the clearing, hissing and snorting, but hold back their fire. They're more enormous by the day, their shoulders now twice his height. Their massive tails are as long as a galloping horse, and their sharp talons longer than his hand.

Minason has grown too, still lean but more muscular and wider in the chest. His confidence has grown too, away from his Da's fists and the torments of the young villagers.

That afternoon Blaze wakes from her nap and lumbers over to where Minason sits under a tree, sketching his Baba as she rests in the shade. He smiles companionably at his magnificent friend as she leans down to nudge him with her snout. He reaches up to scratch her under her chin. "Are you heading out to hunt?"

The young dragon gazes at him with her swirling golden eyes and sends a picture of him flying on her back. <<*MMEEENN-SSSAAN FFFLAAYYY*>> She extends her wing beside him.

Minason's eyes open wide. He puts down his drawing and slowly stands up. He's spent his whole life daydreaming of flying. Except now, he can't keep his knees shaking. Now that there's a chance to actually do it, he's terrified. What if he falls off? What if Blaze isn't strong enough to carry him? He imagines himself hurtling down from the sky.

Blaze huffs and snorts impatiently. <<*MMEEENN-SSSAAN FFFLAAYYY*>>

Trembling, he climbs up her leathery wing, holding on to its edge. Baba calls out in fear, but he resolutely ignores her. He finds a perch at the base of Blaze's neck and straddles between two large spurs on the ridge that extends down most of her back. He holds onto the spur in front of him, careful not to cut himself on its point.

Her muscles bunch under him and she leaps into the sky, her great wings effortlessly lifting them upwards. Minason clings to the spur in front of him and grips her neck with his knees, closing his eyes and trying not to scream. But then Blaze straightens out and circles high above their clearing on Cougar Mountain.

He opens his eyes and looks around in amazement and awe. The sky goes farther than he can see, puffy clouds floating over Raven's Peak across the valley, and what looks like it could be water in the distance. In the other direction, smoke tendrils trail from the peak of Dragon's End. The ravens and falcons are flying far below them. His daydreams of flying were nothing compared to this. He hollers with glee, fear forgotten, and she soars even higher.

She flies him across to the other side of the valley. Spires appear to be growing out of the treetops at the base of Raven's Peak, and the valley is filled with grand colorful tents and banners. He remembers hearing some travelers on the mountain talking about the grand conclave of the Fae, where there is to be a new Queen anointed.

Minason wonders if that's what's going on down there. He leans forward, mouth agape, but he can't see around Blaze's wide neck. He leans sideways to get a better look, and for just a moment one hand lets go of the spur he's been clinging to.

All of a sudden, he's sliding down off the dragon's neck. He grabs for another spur, but he's already slipped away from her spiky ridge and her scales are too smooth to grasp. He tries to grab the edge of her wing, but in his panic he can't find anything to hang on to and his hand slides off. The wind tears the scream out of his mouth as he falls, plunging to a certain death.

Helplessly flailing, he plummets toward the earth, already feeling the horror of being smashed on the rocks below. But suddenly there's a tight band around his waist and his descent is jerked to a halt. It's her giant talons, wrapped firmly around him. Minason is in a daze as she flies him back to their clearing, hanging limply from her grip.

She drops him unceremoniously on the ground and takes off again to hunt for her evening meal. It takes him a long time to stop shaking.

Unnerved, Minason tries to go about their daily business, hardly speaking to Baba, and staying away from the dragons. But a few days later, he builds up his courage and asks her to fly again. Blaze ignores him. The next day he asks again, assuring her he will hang on tight. Blaze snorts disdainfully and nudges him with her snout, knocking him over.

He's too ashamed to tell his Baba what happened, but her observant eye doesn't miss what's going on between her grandson and his beloved dragon. She soon figures out what happened and thinks for a long time, trying to remember something. Then she gets to work. She makes up several wide strips of leather from animal hides, then gathers long grasses, which she twists and wraps into sturdy lengths of rope.

After several days, she emerges from their cave, beaming, with an odd-looking contraption hanging from her hands. Curious, Minason and the dragons gather around her to see what it is. She holds it up to Blaze, and turns to her grandson. "This is for both of you. I copied it from the pictures in the ruin next to our village. It's a harness."

CHAPTER 34

Ylva scurries us into another chamber and silently pulls aside a tapestry, revealing a small niche for us to hide in. She places the Unnoticeable ward on us and quickly leaves the room.

"Venerable Dame, we're searching for the new Queen Designate. She has disappeared and we fear she'll meet the same fate as her cousin Marielle."

"I haven't left my chalet for these last few days. Why are you looking here?"

The captain of the Queen's Guard explains, "She's been seen coming down Cougar Mountain with two others who may be her captors."

"I'll keep her in mind next time I go out. What does she look like?"

"She's a dancer. Tall, with golden curly hair. May we have permission to search your chalet? They may have crept in when you were occupied." She allows them to enter, requesting that they not disturb any of her ancient artifacts.

Attican again. I suppress a snigger, picturing him with the Queen's Guard, stumbling and cursing his way across Queensdale Valley after we drugged their food and freed the dragon, shouting louder after each failed portal.

We hear them searching the parlor we were just sitting in. I wrack my brain, trying to remember if her servant cleared away the platters with our food. They don't make much noise. The Captain gives several quiet commands, then they enter the chamber where we're hiding behind the tapestry.

The Guards look behind and under all the settees and cabinets. We can barely see them through the thick weave. They circle the parlor, examining the Venerable Dame's many wall hangings. Our unwashed clothes and bodies are pungent, and we're squeezed together in the hidden nook. I hold my breath, hoping the glamour concealing us includes the sense of smell. Ours is the last one, and just as they approach us, Gundega barely manages to suppress a sneeze. I almost faint when one of the Guards stops and reaches to pull the tapestry aside, but the Captain is already at the door. He orders them to finish up in here and continue with the rest of the chalet.

It takes forever, but finally we hear Attican thank the Venerable Dame and they leave.

After a long wait, the Venerable Dame pulls back the tapestry and guides us to a different door than the one we came in from. Elena hands us carrysacks full of provisions and closes the door behind her. She leads us along a path curving up around the side of the palace.

The Guards are waiting for us just past the first bend. We don't even have time to react as they seize Caden and Gundega. The Captain more gently takes my arm. He tells Elena to return to the Venerable Dame, explaining that he didn't want to disrupt her home by detaining us there.

"How did you find us?"

"We're trained to see through the Unnoticeable spell, Your Grace, and your party carries the odor of travelers." He says this with a straight face. "Please come this way. Her majesty Queen Maelys is waiting for you. I'm sorry we weren't able to accompany you once we had to leave to find the dragons on Cougar Mountain."

I don't giggle this time.

The captain steers me by the elbow through a grand entrance into the palace. It's a breathtaking structure, crafted over centuries by the most skillful of coaxers. They manipulated countless trees to grow together, to form grand rooms and curving hallways. Looking up, I see it's well ventilated, with plenty of windows and high slits near the tops of rooms. It smells like the forest in a dry summer, with passing whiffs of floral or herbal scents.

The halls bustle with courtiers, messengers, and servants carrying out their business. Will-o'-the-wisps form clusters of light, and in the bigger rooms they gather into elegant chandeliers, lending their gentle radiance into every corner. I glimpse brilliant tapestries and opulent settees, each room differently furnished. Blue, green and silver suggest a pool in the forest, deep purple and red like a cascade of blossoms, bright orange, yellow and green like an orchard.

I want to stop and gawk at every room, but the captain keeps bustling us past magnificent halls, ballrooms, parlors, and rooms whose purpose I can only guess at.

The other Guards lead Caden and Gundega, but not as gently. Caden walks with as much dignity as his situation allows, but Gundega keeps trying to shake off her Guard's firm grip as she limps along beside him. She keeps muttering angrily, her usual croak more like a snarl. I can't hear everything, but from time to time she raises her voice and I hear 'liar,' 'hag,' 'tricked,' and 'cheater.'

They don't bring us to the Queen, but instead to a lavishly furnished drawing room at the end of a wide curving hallway. Attican tells the Guards to wait outside with Caden and Gundega and escorts me in. The room is cluttered with extravagant ornaments, sculptures, and jewelled boxes on every surface. A bald Fae courtier with pale violet eyes and a trim white beard sits behind an overly ornate desk and inspects my dusty travel clothes with an ill-disguised sneer.

"Your Grace, we have been waiting for you these many weeks."

"Who are you, and what do you want? I'm supposed to meet with the Queen."

"All in good time, Your Grace. It's not so much what I want as what you'll want. There are those in the palace who would try to lead you and the Queendom astray. I will assist you and guide you as you learn to rule the land."

"Thank you, but I still don't know who you are or what you want."

"Lord Jarin, Your Grace, at your service. I am Lord Chamberlain to the Queen." He stands up and walks toward me, insisting that I take a seat. He hands me a cup of hibiscus mead, which he says is the favorite of Queen Maelys.

"Young Sislie—you don't mind if I call you Sislie, do you—you have so much to learn, and little time before the Grand

Conclave, and Her Majesty is busy with her pressing duties. I am here to help you."

His condescending demeanor insults me, and his oily voice and manner are repulsive. And the hibiscus mead carries a whiff of something that reminds me of the porridge at Gundega's cottage. I pretend to touch the cup to my lips as he lectures me on the importance of keeping the Land safe from forces outside and within.

I sit and listen for as long as I can, but I have pressing business too. I jump out of my chair, spilling the hibiscus mead onto his carpet, and try to speak in a haughty voice. "Lord Jarin, I urgently need to see the Queen. Please take me to her."

He frowns but nods to Attican, who guides us down another long curving passage until we arrive at a large hall whose walls are hung with glowing tapestries.

Jarin scowls as they leave the room. He barks at the servant who has been standing beside his desk. "See to it that assistant cook has her meals prepared as I instructed. See to it personally."

An ancient Fae sits scowling on a bejewelled and elaborately carved throne atop a raised dais. She's surrounded by courtiers, all wearing fine gowns, waistcoats and smirks as they look us over, in our worn and stained travel clothes.

The Queen is tiny, and so thin that her bony skeleton almost shines through her skin. Her eyes are also small, a gleaming deep purple, almost black. Her mouth forms a thin line. Her purple brocade gown and matching feathered headpiece are bejewelled, and I wonder how she can carry such a weighty mass. Also, she wears a Youthfulness glamour, which the courtiers surrounding her appear to accept, though being Fae, they obviously can see through it.

She gives us a bored and disdainful look as the captain announces, "Your Magnificence, I present Her Grace, the Queen Designate Sislie, come to prepare for her anointing."

The Guards, Caden and I all kneel before the Queen, but Gundega is defiant. Her Guard has to push her down, forcing her to comply.

"And here is young Caden from the Human town," says the Queen in a stiletto voice that makes me clench my teeth, "having successfully accomplished the task I set him to."

Caden goes to reply, but a tall courtier standing next to the Queen moves his fingers in a peculiar way and Caden remains silent, merely bowing his head. My suspicions are briefly aroused again, but I remember it's not all as it seems. I should be relieved, safely among my own kind again, but I'm filled with dread and foreboding. I glance around the hall. My parents should be here, but there's nobody I know. This whole situation is so strange, so contradictory. I don't know who I can trust, or whether someone from here sent an assassin. I'm surrounded by those who wish to use me for unknown purposes.

CHAPTER 35

Lord Jarin bustles in and takes a place standing next to the Queen, opposite the courtier who signaled to Caden. The Queen barely glances at me, and she doesn't speak to me. She orders her Guards to take me to guest quarters, to be made presentable. I'd be insulted if I didn't know how unkempt I look.

Lord Jarin leans toward her, his voice fawning, "Your Majesty, Lady Tyra would be an exemplary guide and companion for the young Queen Designate."

But the other courtier contradicts him. "Benevolence, might I suggest Mistress Liana as a better choice? She is the most experienced of your handmaidens, and could help Her Grace learn palace deportment, as well as caring for her needs."

Jarin scowls and gives him a surly look as the Queen flicks her fingers at one of the handmaidens, who hurries out of the room.

As they escort me from the chamber, I almost trip when I hear her thank Caden for bringing me, and order her Lord Chamberlain to pay him his reward. Walking down the long corridor with the Guards, I'm full of contradictory thoughts vying for my attention. *Is he a liar after all? Did he accept the reward? Why didn't she speak to me? Who is that Lord Jarin and what does he want from me? Why aren't my parents here? But his eyes are so in inviting. Is he just pretending?*

The Guards escort me to a luxurious apartment, consisting of a richly appointed drawing room, sleeping chamber, dressing room, and privy. It's much bigger than the simply furnished rooms I left behind in my Clan's tree village with its swaying ladders and rope walkways. Like the rest of the palace, the walls in my rooms were formed long ago by coaxers who beguiled the trees to shape themselves into these buildings and halls. The walls are hung with fine tapestries, and the drawing room contains several ornate settees, cabinets, chairs and a small desk.

I look around. I suppose I'd better get used to the finery, if I'm going to be Queen. I try to muster my resolve, but I'm still exhausted, and too weighed down by my destiny. I'm haunted by what I saw in the Venerable Dame's tapestry, terrified that I won't save the Land.

I stand in the middle of the elaborately furnished rooms, bleak and alone. All I can hear is the Guards' voices, talking quietly on the other side of the door. They have someone to talk with. I don't. I'm isolated. Overwhelmed. I miss my village, my family, my cousins, my fellow dancers. Caden. Even Gundega. My throat clenches and unbidden tears flood my eyes. I collapse on the elegant bed in my soot-stained clothes and sob into the ornately embroidered pillow.

I don't get enough privacy to have a really good cry, but I'm mostly finished when there's a brief knock at the door. The handmaiden from the throne room enters, followed by burly porters bearing a large vat of steaming water and two servants with a stack of towels. I hastily wipe the tears from my puffy eyes.

The handmaiden ignores my soot-streaked cheeks and helps me off with my clothing, and into the vat. Even though I'm feeling distressed, it's been a long time since I've been able to bathe, and it feels good to sink into the lavender scented water. The servants rub a generous portion of suds into my hair, scrub me down, massage me, groom my nails, and dry me off with thick towels. When they're done, the handmaiden brings me a courtly dress from one of the wardrobes. I ask for something plainer, and she finds one in the wardrobe that's a bit less ornate, but not much. She helps me into it.

"Please sit here, Your Grace, and I will dress your hair."

For a moment, I don't realize she's addressing me. Then I laugh, because all my curly hair ever needs is a towel and a bit of fluffing. But then I remember how Marielle always teased me about my fluffy head, and the giggle dies in my throat. It was Marielle, with her long dark hair, who should be here getting her hair brushed, not me.

For the first time I actually look at the handmaiden. She's almost as tall as me, her face framed by a crown of braids the color of young pine cones. She wears a simple embroidered gown of rough silk dyed a pale sky blue.

"I'm no kind of Grace, I'm just Sislie. Please call me Sislie. What's your name?"

"I'm Liana, Your Grace, um, Sislie, on rotation from the Squirrel Clan to serve the Queen. She bids me attend to your needs."

"Thank you Liana. There's probably nothing you can do for my hair, but I'm hungry. All I've eaten lately has been trail food and a few tiny cakes at the Venerable Dame's home. Can you get me a proper meal?"

"I can, Your... Sislie." she turns to the servants gathering my bathing supplies and dirty clothing. "Please bring refreshments for the Queen-in-waiting. Bring plenty. She is hungry."

I like the look of this handmaiden. She's just a few years older than me, and the only lady of the court I've seen not wearing a haughty smirk. "Liana, can you help me? I was supposed to study for this, according to the rules of succession, but never before has a Queen-to-be died, and I was only ever interested in dancing, so I mostly ignored my studies. I know so little about the court, or the responsibilities of the Queen."

Liana fetches a small stool and sits beside me. "Sislie, we were all horrified and grieved at the death of Marielle, and the court has been in chaos ever since. I'll help you in any way I can. You do have friends here. You'll meet them soon."

"I'm wretchedly ignorant. I don't even know who to bow to."

Liana's placid demeanor broadens into a wide grin. "Oh, that's the easiest part. You bow to nobody except the Queen, and everyone else bows to you. Oh my, you really don't...." She's interrupted by a knock on the door as the servants return, carrying a large platter mounded with breads, cakes, berries and nuts, sweet honey wine, and an elegant tureen of soup. They place it on a finely wrought table in the drawing room and leave the apartment at Liana's gesture.

The food smells wonderful and my stomach is growling. I reach for a bowl of soup, but something makes me hesitate.

There's a faint whiff of something that reminds me of the hibiscus mead Lord Jarin gave me, and Gundega's porridge. I look up at Liana. She's holding up her hand and looking at me with a guarded expression on her face.

"What is this?" I ask.

She comes closer to smell the food. "You probably wouldn't have noticed if you weren't a healer. It's an herb meant to soften your will. I don't know why it's in your food, but I expect Queen Maelys wants you to be more susceptible to her glamours."

We inspect each item on the platter. The soup is tainted, and the breads, but the cakes seem clear, as do the berries and honey wine. I gobble some of them down, but I can't live on wine and cakes. I ask her, "Could I have some spring water please, and could you find me some nut breads that are not tainted?" We pour the soup down the privy and mess up the platter so it looks like some of it's been eaten.

Liana goes in search of food. I'm reassured by her forthrightness and hope I can trust her. I need a friend to help me maneuver through this twisting maze of a court. Meanwhile, I explore my rooms. There are a few simple gowns among the finery in the wardrobes, but most of them are impossibly ornate. Even the smallclothes are lavishly embroidered and ribboned.

Liana returns with the servants, who take away the remains of the platter. She reaches into the folds of her gown and pulls out a small package containing a loaf of nut bread. Her deep pocket yields a slim carafe of water with a cork stopper. "I'll try to bring you some food every day, but we have to be careful that nobody notices. Some of your servants are spies for Queen Maelys. She wants to keep you sequestered while you prepare for your anointing, and the Guards at your door aren't necessarily to be trusted."

We're interrupted by voices at the door, and a knock. Liana opens it to the tall courtier who signaled to Caden in the Queen's parlor. We inspect each other. A courtier by his clothing, but his wide muscular frame suggests a warrior. He wears an elegant scabbard and his elven-crafted sword has a finely wrought hilt. Liana introduces him as Lord Kairon, consort to Queen Maelys, advisor to the Clans, and friend to the Rangers.

I look at her intently, and she nods. "Lord Kairon is a trusted friend and ally. He'll keep you safe and help you prepare for the ceremony. Afterward...."

"Your Grace, we don't have much time." He bows hastily. "I've sent your door guards on an errand, but they'll be back soon and meanwhile there's someone who urgently needs to see you."

I burst into tears as my mother rushes into the room, my father close behind. "Oh Mama, I'm so sorry. This is all my fault." It all tumbles out, words tripping over each other. "I was dancing in the glade and I got kidnapped and sleeping powder and there was a forest fire and we rescued Caden and hid in the tunnels and we saved a dragon and the Venerable Dame told us everything and I'm sorry, I'm so sorry, I don't know if I can do this."

My parents hug and kiss me and hold me for a long time. My mother the healer wipes her eyes and then checks me over.

"You were drugged, Sislie, and you were in the dwarf tunnels for such a long time. That's why we couldn't locate you. Most of it is out of your system by now. Let me see if there's anything else." She gently cradles my face, then places her hands on my shoulders to feel for any wrongness. "Other than a few bruises, you seem to be well." She takes a pouch from the many small pockets of her cloak and hands it to Liana. "Give her this clover tea."

She turns back to me. "The clover will finish cleansing any remaining traces of sleeping powder, and it will help you clarify your thinking. We want to hear everything, but it will have to be later, because the Queen wants to keep you isolated and we don't have much time."

She gestures to Lord Kairon. "You've never met him, because he's been at court since before you were born, but Kairon is from our Clan. He is a good friend. You can trust him absolutely. But we can't stay. Be strong, my precious daughter. You are brave and smart, and we know you can do this."

Footsteps and the rattle of arms outside the door interrupt her. Kairon says to them, "Can you *flicker* out past the Guards?" I reach out to my parents again, but they vanish from sight.

Kairon opens the door to the Guards. "Caden has not escaped, Sire. He's with Ned."

"Ned is one of the Queen's spies," says Kairon after he closes the door and turns back into the room. "Caden has no doubt been sent to give him any information he may have about those supposed dragons. She's been obsessed with them. And he's probably been instructed to recruit him as a spy."

Another wave of mistrust floods me and again my heart tightens in my chest. *I'll just have to forget about him if he's going to be a spy for the Queen. Oh right. That will be me in a few days. What will I do then? I'll think about this later. Is there a dungeon in the palace?*

I decide to check with Kairon. "Do you know Caden? He's a half-Fae Ranger from the Human village that claims was coming to rescue me, but it turns out he might have been working for the Queen. I wonder if he helped the Guards capture us."

A trace of discomfort passes over his face before he answers. "Your Grace, one of my responsibilities is to maintain our relationship with the Humans. So yes, I am aware of him. He's very honorable by reputation, as are all the Rangers. I'd be most surprised if he turned out to be untrustworthy."

He starts to say more, but I interrupt him. "Ok. What's important now is preparing for the Grand Conclave. And please don't call me Grace. My name is Sislie. If you're going to be my trusted advisor, you should call me Sislie."

My mother's tea is already working. My mind is clearing. I even feel like I'm growing on the inside as I contemplate the enormous task ahead of me. The ceremony is coming too soon, and I decide right then and there that I'm going to forget about Caden. I have more important things to think about.

"Sislie, then. But please, only among ourselves. The palace is full of intrigue, and until you learn who to trust, we should stick with the more formal address: Your Grace, Mistress Liana, Lord Kairon. Be especially cautious when you meet Lord Jarin and his coterie. The wellbeing of the Queendom is not their primary concern."

"I've already met him. He had me brought to him before I saw the Queen. I know I'll have to learn about all that, but the Grand Conclave is almost here. I need to study for that."

"I understand you've met with the Venerable Dame Ylva. We'll get her to you over these last few days. She can instruct you in the things I don't know about. But meanwhile, I can teach you what I know of the rites and ceremonies of your anointing."

Kairon instructs me for the next couple of hours, giving me an overview of the four days of processions, ceremonies, speeches, presentations, and dedications. But it's been a long day, and even with the clover tea clearing my mind and my parent's visit giving me courage, I'm overloaded and can't take in much. I'll start memorizing my speeches and dedications tomorrow.

After he takes his leave, Liana and the servants return with another platter of food and wine. She dismisses the servants, and again we inspect each item on the platter, setting aside the tainted custard and flans. She has brought me fresh spring water and more of the tasty nut bread she brought earlier. She helps me out of my gown and into my nightdress. I fall into the soft bed, spent. She spreads a coverlet over me, made of dandelion down and brightly colored feathers, and takes her leave.

I'm exhausted but still overwhelmed and I can't fall asleep. I toss and turn and keep seeing the tunnels and the forest fire. The dragons swooping down on the Guards. The look in Caden's eyes, the delicious feelings I had for him curdling into suspicion as I hear Maelys' brittle voice promising his reward. My thoughts keep churning. Kairon tells me he's reliable. I wish I could trust him. I wish Marielle was still alive. I wish I could hug my mother again. Finally, the exhaustion takes me and I slide down into sleep.

A soft scraping noise and a thump intrude into my troubled dream of hiding in the tunnels. The Guards have found us. I startle awake. It takes me a minute to register a dark figure looming over the foot of my bed. I jump up and make a hasty ball of light just as the figure holds up a hand to gesture silence. It's Caden.

He stops me on the way to the door. "Please, I need to see to you."

"She thanked you. She rewarded you." I want to shout, Kairon's reassurance forgotten. "Get out of here or I'll call the Guards."

"That's not what you thought when we saved the dragon, was it?" He reaches for me, but I shake his hand off my shoulder and he crosses his arms, frowning. "Why do you keep getting so suspicious?"

I don't know why. It's just that I'm anxious and jumpy. And I like him too much. But I need to focus on learning to be Queen. I don't have time for this charming and capable half-Human with gorgeous eyes. I need to keep my distance. I try to muster my resolve, but I can't keep from looking at him.

He stands gazing at me, his scowl gradually fading. "Sislie, I just want to love you and help you. I understand if you have to be a maiden Queen…"

"No, no, it's nothing like that. The Fae are quite relaxed about lovemaking and romance. It's just that I have to concentrate on my training, and becoming Queen. There's so much to learn and only a few days to get it right."

I intend to step away from him, but instead I lean forward and he slides his arms around me. "Oh Caden," I moan into his chest, "I feel like I can't catch my breath. I don't know if I can do this."

He holds me and strokes my cheek. "Sislie, Sislie, you're strong, and intelligent and capable. You'll be a great queen. I know you will. You will heal the Land. You will get wiser as time goes by."

He ignores my protestations and guides me back to my bed. He reclines and leans against the headboard, taking me in his arms. He strokes my back, rocking me like a child, nuzzling my hair and murmuring soft words as I sink into exhausted sleep.

CHAPTER 36

In the morning, I wake up at first light. Caden is still sleeping, his breath steady and slow. I snuggle into his shoulder, enjoying the soft bed, his clean, manly smell and the comfort of his arms. He stretches and sighs and pulls me closer. He nuzzles my hair and kisses my forehead, then starts to work his way down toward my lips. That tantalizing hot sensation swells throughout my body and I turn to him, this time trusting whatever may be and eager to taste more of what we've only sampled.

Just then, a soft knock on the door announces Liana's arrival. We disentangle as she slips in quietly and stops, trying not to stare.

"Excuse me, Your Grace." She turns to leave.

"No, stop, wait. Liana, you have to meet Caden.

Liana curtsies awkwardly. I chuckle at the look on her face as she watches Caden get up from the bed, still fully dressed from last night. He bows to her. "Lady, I'm pleased to make your acquaintance. I am one of the Rangers that patrol the mountains around Queensdale Valley."

She scrutinizes him intently. "I remember you. You're related to Moriko, the weaver from First Bend. And we also met that other time on the path, with the Queen."

"Yes, Lady, when she tried to recruit me. But I was looking for Sislie, anyway." He dives under the bed as another knock announces servants bearing my warm wash water and a platter of fresh fruit, pudding and biscuits.

After they leave, he rolls out from under the bed and Liana takes me into the dressing room for hasty ablutions and another dress that's still too ornate for my taste. There's enough on the platter for both of us, but she warns Caden not to eat until we inspect the food. She teaches him to check for that faint odor, in case he is given tainted food as well.

"We can tell Caden everything," I say with my first mouthful of apricot, "and Caden. We need to hear what has been happening with you. Where have you been?" I lean toward him. It's all I can do to keep my hand from touching him.

"She sent Gundega and me to meet with her spy, Ned. He's really creepy."

Liana interjects, "Ned is a broken, or spoilt Fae. He was injured at the time of fledging, so his wing nubs never developed. That's why he looks so old. Fae who lose their birthright age much faster than the rest of us, and have a shorter lifespan, unless they avoid using all spells or glamours, which is very unlikely for anyone who can do them at all."

"Like Gundega."

"Yes. But that doesn't explain why Ned is so detestable. Nobody understands why Queen Maelys keeps him around. She uses him to spy, and for personal errands. Except for that, he reports to Jarin, her Lord Chamberlain, who's involved in his own schemes. What did he want with you?"

"He had a lot of questions about the tunnels, especially if there was any evidence of treasures. He thought there were magical objects to be found."

Magical objects. I wonder if the green stone I found is one of these. My hand wanders into my pocket and I feel its slight warmth.

"We told him we had stumbled into them by accident, and basically know nothing. Then he asked about the dragons and their keepers. He kept quizzing me about Minason, a young fellow from the Asmung village that I've met once or twice on patrol. He thinks Minason is the keeper of the dragons. He offered us wine, which had some of the same smell as this food.

"While we were talking, he was summoned to Lord Jarin. They left me to my own devices, but they took Gundega to work in the kitchens."

"Stay away from Jarin." Liana interrupts. "We don't trust him. He spurs on the Queen's harshest and most greedy impulses. He wants to turn the Queendom into a martial state. Kairon does his best to stop his schemes, but the Queen is getting worse and Kairon has been losing his influence.

"She's not always clear in her mind. She spends more energy adding to her royal menagerie and holding grand balls than caring for her Queendom. It was because of her that Marielle had such a small escort when she was killed. Most of her Honor Guard had been put to work moving the Queen's treasures out of the Royal Treasury where they belong, and into her private stronghold."

I'm staggered by this news. Our most horrible tragedy, all for some disgusting trinkets. How can someone be so corrupt, so greedy? How can a Queen...? My misgivings about her curdles into hatred and for once I'm glad I'm going to replace her. No, not hatred, but steely resolve. I can do better than this, I will do better than this. The Queendom needs someone who will love and care for the Land and the Fae and all who share her. I might not have wanted to be Queen, but I'll be the best Queen I can.

This day is full of lessons with Kairon and the Venerable Ylva, and the Lord Chamberlain Jarin, whose unctuous voice and manner make my flesh crawl.

And fittings. Endless fittings. The Grand Conclave lasts a fiveday—three days of celebration and dedications, then one day for pledges of fealty and anointing the new queen. On the last day, I go to my special duties and the Clan elders gather to deliberate.

The first three days, Her Grace has to wear a different gown each day. And a different headdress. I sometimes used to have costumes fitted as a dancer, but they were always simple, and flowing. This parade of silks, chiffons, brocades, and frothy laces—each one jewelled and beribboned, each one more elaborate than the last—is beyond tedious. And it takes hours.

I do my best to maintain decorum with the seamstresses, who might also be spying for the Queen, but the torture of the milliners is almost unbearable. They brush and pull my unruly hair, twisting, braiding, and pinning it into submission. Then they cram my head into the tiniest of caps that will hold the headdress. It gives me a headache. They try to insist that's how it has to be, and when I threaten to refuse to wear any headdress at all, they offer to cut my hair so it won't take up so much space. Finally I yell at them, and they scurry away, returning with a slightly larger cap, which they insist is not as good, because the concoctions of feathers and jewels are heavy and must not slip. But I'm willing to submit to it.

At last, the fittings are done and the gown-making party takes their leave with many bows and apologies to Her Grace, and reassurances that the final adjustments will take hardly any time at all.

Worst are the lessons from Lord Chamberlain Jarin. He is attended by his niece, Lady Tyra, who gives me the barest curtsy and avoids looking at me. But she hangs on every word he says, as though the lesson were for her, and not for me.

He manages to combine both fawning and condescension in his slimy voice, as he presents his version of the state of the Queendom. It's wildly different from Kairon's. He informs me the Queendom is under imminent threat by unnamed forces from overseas and our resources should be dedicated to building a fleet of ships so we can sail to defeat them. He assures me that he will help me succeed in this once I am Queen, and that I must trust him. He hints that Kairon is disloyal to the Land, and possibly even in the pay of those same unnamed overseas forces.

By the time he's been with me for an hour, I want to scream. It's all I can do to keep a decorous performer's expression on my face as he keeps explaining that I'm not to worry, and that I'll understand these things when I'm older.

Kairon does his best to keep Jarin away, flattering him and keeping him distracted with problems having to do with preparations for the Grand Conclave. But I keep wondering what kind of schemes he is working, and why that niece, Tyra, is always sitting in on the lessons. Liana manages to persuade him that I have many headaches that leave me unable to receive him most of the time. We have to keep up this subterfuge with the servants too, because we don't always know which ones are spies. So keeping me sequestered turns out to be useful after all because that way hardly anyone is permitted to call on me.

CHAPTER 37

Liana and I are inspecting my supper when we hear a thump from my sleeping chamber. Caden peers around the door, pretending to be stealthy, and skulks into the drawing room, making a shifty eyed face that has us all laughing for the first time all day.

He is followed by our little bobcat, Spark, who is not such a tiny kitten anymore. She hops up on the table to see if there's any food for her, too. "Gundega's room by the kitchen is too small to keep her there. She thought Spark would keep you company and warn you in case of trouble while you're sleeping. Like in the cave that time."

"How did you get in here?" Liana's voice is lighthearted, but she's frowning slightly and I can see that she's concerned to see him come into my chamber so easily.

"I've been scouting. Sensing. Sneaking. Exploring the palace and finding places to hide. This whole place is honeycombed with secret passages between many of the chambers." He ignores Liana's raised eyebrow. "A lot of them are too narrow to get through, because the coaxed trees have kept growing very slowly, even after the building was complete. But I found this handy little corridor that goes almost from the kitchens to these chambers." He pulls out a bundle from under his cape with a flourish. "Gundega sends her greetings, and some dainties you'll enjoy."

We tuck in to some delicious pies full of winter vegetables cooked with aromatic herbs, and a small crock of untainted soup. It's the best meal I've had since I got here. Caden and I share the flask of honey wine, and he shares what he's learned from the servants and by eavesdropping on Jarin and his coterie. None of it is good. The Queen's obsession with dragons has everyone mystified, preparations for the Grand Conclave are in disarray, and Lady Tyra keeps acting as though she's the next Queen.

After the servants clear away the remains of the meal, and Caden slides out from under my bed, Liana looks at him meaningfully and offers that it's time for them to take their leave.

"Thanks, Liana, you can go ahead. Caden and I have some things to discuss. I'll see you in the morning." I'm sitting with Spark cuddled up on my lap, and put on my most nonchalant face as she leaves us, glancing over her shoulder as she exits past the Guard.

Caden scratches Spark behind the ear, then gently takes her off my lap. He takes my hand with an enticing smile, pulls me to my feet, and tugs me toward the sleeping chamber.

"Wait, Caden, we really do need to talk."

"What would you like to talk about?" He slides his arms around me and draws me close. "We can talk in there."

What I really want to do is press against him for more of what I've only had a nibble of. But instead, I place my hands on his chest and push him to arm's length. "Caden, I really like you, but you know I'm promised to the Land. Everything's going to be different after the Grand Conclave. I might be different. I don't understand all the anointing rites and enchantments, and the next day I go on to that sacred grotto to receive the elixir from the sleeping god."

"Sislie, I know." He picks up my hands and holds them to his lips. "I've had a lot of time to think about this since we got here. I've never said it before, because it sounds crazy, but as soon as I heard your name, I felt my destiny calling. And then I saw you in that vision before I came to look for you. I loved you right then. All I want is to love you. And care for you. Once you're Queen I'll be yours in any way I can."

"I don't know, Caden, I don't want to hurt you." I try to pull back but I feel reassured just having him near and my traitorous feet take me a step closer.

"I don't either, but we don't know what's in the future." His eyes warm and entice me, his lips murmur the words of invitation. "I'm willing to take the chance. Just let me be with you."

Suddenly, my doubts and worries slide away. It feels right to lean into him. We stand holding each other for a long moment. But then the heat flares between us and comfort kindles into passion.

We slowly make our way to the sleeping chamber, kissing, touching, undoing buttons and ties. Silken gown, leather jerkin, trousers, slippers, and boots somehow collapse on the floor. The smallclothes trip us up and we fall giggling onto my soft queenly bed. We roll and tumble, laughing, kissing, tasting, exploring.

But just before my hand locates his proud manhood, he stops, looking serious.

"Are you sure? I have no sheath."

"It's ok. It's not my time. Fae are fertile only when we choose to, so we could never have an uninvited pregnancy." My smile and eyes and hands give him the answer he's looking for.

His lips and teeth tickle my tingling nipples as his fingers entertain the curves of my back. When they find my wing nubs, I groan and arch my back. Delighted, he strokes and teases them, making me moan and writhe. I have to keep from crying out lest the Guards hear me as he follows his tongue down a slow trail to investigate me at his leisure. He keeps me moaning at the brink of ecstasy for the longest time, then slowly detonates the explosion of bliss that surges through my body. Then again, and again.

He leans on his elbow, watching me recover, a pleased smile playing at the corner of his lips. I reach up and trace his jawline with my finger, then pull him toward me and into me. When we join, it feels right. "Caden," I whisper his name as the momentum intensifies. He calls out my name when the irresistible wave takes him.

Afterward, we nuzzle and hold each other, sleepy and content. "Tell me about these bumpy ridges along your shoulder blades," he asks with laughing eyes, titillating one with his finger and making me shiver, "Special pleasure zones of the Fae?"

"Yes, and no. They're wing nubs. Most Humans never see them, but the Fae have wings, which we use in various ways. They're the primary source of our power. They draw on the quintessential Aether, or cosmic energy. And they're also pleasure zones, as you have so artfully discovered." I grin, and shiver at the memory.

"But not for flying, I've heard."

"But not for flying, though I don't know why that is."

"May I see them?"

"Yes, but another time. I need to recover from the exertions you put me through."

He gives me a lecherous grin and pulls me close. We kiss and nuzzle until we fall asleep in a warm tangle of arms and legs, sheltered this night from the intrigues of the palace.

CHAPTER 38

"Lord Chamberlain, I'm pleased to see you." Kairon bows slightly to Jarin in the curving hallway, hiding his distaste for the aged courtier. "I require your assistance in making some decisions about the Grand Conclave."

Jarin returns the bow with a minimum of respect and invites Kairon into his lavishly furnished drawing room. He offers him a seat at the ornate table and brusquely orders a servant to bring them some refreshment.

"Lord Kairon, you must do something about that halfbreed running around the palace. It's unseemly to have him roaming the halls."

Kairon maintains his calm expression, though he always has to stifle a grimace when he hears the smarmy voice. "Of course, but I expect tolerating, or even befriending him will help to keep you in good standing with the new Queen."

"It might, but I don't like it. It's ill-advised, and could become scandalous. Bad enough, we have to put up with that broken Fae who traveled with her."

"I'm sure I can find something to keep him occupied."

"Fine. Try to keep him out of sight. But more important, what do you know about these supposed dragons? What has Her Majesty told you about them?"

"I know nothing about them. She seems to be keeping that information to herself. I've asked her several times, but she's evasive and ill-tempered if I try to press her. Do you have any clues?"

"Nothing." Jarin is chagrined that Queen Maelys hasn't confided in him. But at least she has told nothing to Kairon, his long-time rival, either. "It's so unusual. She always has my ear. But for once I'm mystified."

They confer about the Conclave, Jarin objecting to the expense of hosting the throng of Clans gathering in the Dale. Kairon points out to him that this will help ensure their loyalty after the anointing. He flatters Jarin about his skillful supervision of the preparations and receptions for Clan leaders during this time.

After Kairon leaves, Jarin mutters to his back, "You won't be so patronizing when I'm in control." He closes the door, then takes a tiny key from a pocket in his waistcoat. He unlocks an ornate cabinet and takes out a tiny blue glass vial with a cork stopper. He examines it, then tucks it back into the cabinet, locking it again. He hurries down the hall to the throne room, a thin smile on his lips.

CHAPTER 39

Liana hurries into their usual meeting place in a rarely used morning room. The normally unflappable Kairon is pacing around the room. He stops abruptly when she arrives, but stands scowling, fiddling with his scabbard and straightening his waistcoat.

"What's wrong? What happened?" She refrains from rushing to his side.

"It's my son, Liana. He's in the palace, with Sislie."

"Caden? He's your son?"

"Yes." He continues pacing again, his hands marking the rhythm of his words. "It's been a secret all these years. We couldn't let Maelys find out. He probably hates me. I couldn't be a real father. I could only watch from a distance. I've helped him in small ways, with anonymous gifts and assistance that wouldn't be attributed to me. Moriko knows...." His voice trails off and he gazes into the distance.

"My dear Kairon," she says, stepping closer and taking his hands in hers, "He couldn't possibly hate you. You are the hope of the Queendom. The Queen's abuses and Jarin's scheming would have destroyed us long ago without you."

"Yes, but he wouldn't know about any of that." He absently withdraws his hands from hers, oblivious to the momentary disappointment in her eyes. "Nor would he be aware of the gifts. I always made sure they seemed to come from Moriko, or one of her friends."

"It must have been awful."

He looks at his trusted confidant. "It would be best not to mention anything, Liana. We need to concentrate on getting Sislie to the Grand Conclave."

"I know it normally wouldn't matter who she takes as a lover, but you should know he's often in her quarters, and they have slept together at least once."

"Oh damn. Surely she knows she can't...."

"I know. It would even be complicated to have him stay in the palace. And Jarin would take advantage of that to cause trouble."

"Yes, he would. But we'll have to deal with that later." They sit down at the writing table where they usually confer, and Kairon continues. "I'm worried about the Queen. She's ignoring Sislie when she ought to be teaching her. We can work around that, but for once I can't tell what she's plotting. Half of her Guards are scouring the land in search of those dragons, if that's what they really are. Living dragons would usher in a whole new era for us. I've tried to talk with her about it, but she brushes me off. Do you have any clue?"

"Not really, but she got all excited about some ancient scrolls after she first heard Ned's report about those flying creatures." Liana describes what she witnessed from her peephole.

"But hunt them? She can't want them for her menagerie. Besides, if the rumors are accurate, they're growing so fast they'll soon be too big to be contained. Even Jarin is perplexed by her fixation. And after that escapade with her Guards and the Shore-landers…" He raises his eyebrows and allows a smile to curl the corners of his lips. "That was a mighty tantrum, wasn't it? It must have taken those poor wisps days to venture back out from behind the tapestries."

"Did you see the ladies trying to cover their ears," she giggles, "pretending to adjust their headpieces? I thought the old Lord Chamberlain was going to fall over from the blast."

They take the moment of levity, a short break from their responsibilities. Liana is only a handmaiden, but she is highly intelligent. She inherited her mother's network of spies from when she had been the Queen's handmaiden. They rely on her trusted housekeepers, chambermaids, cooks and cleaners, to keep them informed about the Queen, Jarin, and his courtiers.

When they're finished, she tries to reassure him. "I'll do my best to keep Caden out of your way. I expect Sislie's parents won't be pleased about their relationship either."

"You're right. I'll be seeing them shortly. They are trusted friends and advisors. I need them here at the palace, and of course they should be here for Sislie's Grand Conclave."

CHAPTER 40

"I haven't been out of this apartment for days—I feel like a prisoner."

Caden lounges on the settee, admiring her as she performs her stretches. He savors the casual intimacy, though he realizes it won't last long. "Yeah, me too. Maybe we can get you outdoors for an afternoon, or a tour of the secret passages." Though with all the Guards around, and her busy schedule, he's not too hopeful.

There's a short series of knocks at the door, and Kairon comes in with two aristocratic-looking Fae he's never seen before. He leaps to his feet.

"Mother and father, meet my Ranger friend Caden. He's been my companion since the forest fire, and rescued the dragon with me. Caden, you've already met Lord Kairon. These are my parents, Lady Nerysa and Lord Torin."

"We don't meet many half-Humans," says Sislie's mother coming closer. "Which of your parents is Fae?"

"My father, Lady Nerysa, though I don't know who he is." He barely suppresses the bitterness in his voice.

"Then, by the look of your eyes, your mother must be the weaver, Moriko. She once made me an excellent cloak," she says with a gentle smile and reaches out to Caden, "Let me make sure you don't have any lingering effects after that forest fire." He cautiously steps forward, and she places her hands on either side of his head and looks into his eyes. "You seem to be well; I expect my daughter has healed you."

She closes her eyes and pauses a long moment, "But Caden, you carry the essence of our Clan, we appear to be kin, though not close. Wait...."

She releases Caden and steps back, looking sharply at Kairon. "Kairon, how can this be?"

Kairon is alarmed at the unexpected revelation. But he composes himself and turns to Caden. "I didn't want it to come out like this, but you'd have found out, eventually. Caden. Your mother and I, we loved each other. We still love each other. I am your father."

The room goes still. Caden furrows his brows in confusion, as though reacting to a joke he doesn't get. His throat clenches. He looks at Kairon, at Lady Nerysa, back at Kairon. He chokes out, "You're my father?"

"Son, it broke my heart, but I needed to protect you. I'm the Royal Consort. The Queen is jealous and vindictive, even though there's no love between us. If she knew, she'd have brought harm to you or your mother." He takes a step toward Caden, reaching out his hand.

Caden refuses his hand, instead clenching his fists. His eyes harden and his voice is cold. "What do you mean, you love my mother? You abandoned us. She's been alone my entire life."

"No, Caden. I've loved you both in secret all these years. I've watched over you and helped you in any way I could."

"You never watched over us. You were never there. When I was a child, the other kids sneered at me. Townsfolk whispered behind my mother's back. I despise you. I've always hated you." His face flushes and he lunges forward, but Torin holds him back.

Kairon stands in place, eyes miserable. "It's been agony to see you grow up without me. But I've always kept track of you, believe me. I was so proud when you became the youngest Ranger. I wish it had been different. And I wish it could be different now. But unfortunately, it still must remain a secret, at least until after the Grand Conclave."

Caden glares at his Fae father with rage and disbelief. He's not so noble, this important Royal Consort. Years of hurt and resentment burst out of his mouth. "I'll keep your secret, you useless slacker. I don't want it known, anyway. You spent your time lording and feasting at the palace while my mother struggled to build a life for us. When I see her I'll tell her I've met you, for what little it's worth."

He stomps off, angrily pushing past the startled Guard stationed at the door.

Caden uses his Ranger discipline to steel his posture, and manages to contain his fury as he surges down the hall to one of the side entrances of the palace. He keeps his eyes looking straight ahead. He needs to get away from this so-called father, and the elegance of the palace is suddenly cloying. He needs to be in the woods. He needs to hit something, or run, or chop wood, or anything to burn off this overwhelming rage.

Near the exit, a small group of young courtiers and Guards are lounging in the hall, laughing. "Yeah, and that halfbreed bodyguard of hers. They say he's a Ranger—suppose they all dress like yokels?"

"Did you get a load of that hag travelling with her? Another spoilt Fae? She looks like some kind of failed coaxer experiment. Maybe she'll get a job mucking out the Queen's menagerie."

"I hear she's really a dancer. I'll bet her head is as full of fluff on the inside as the outside." The laughter swells. "Some Queen she's going to be."

"Apparently Jarin says she's completely untrained, and he expects her to be a good puppet." The smirking voice continues, "I wonder if she's a good puppet between the sheets."

Caden tries to stride past, determined to ignore them. But when he hears them mock Sislie, his rage boils over. Suddenly, time stops and all of his anger erupts out of his fists. He's on top of the smirking courtier, pummeling the face that mocked Sislie. "Take it back, you piece of kack! You don't deserve to mention her name."

The two Guards in the party laughingly pull him off the young courtier, ignoring his struggles and protestations. They march him down a long hallway to a military-looking side room where their captain is working at his desk. "We caught this one brawling, sir."

The Captain barely glances at him. "Throw him in a cell and let him sleep it off. It's too early in the day to be that much into the mead."

Ignoring his shouted protests, they drag Caden down to a cell below the palace, contained by the roots of its trees. He tries to shout, but the warden casually traces a triangular glamour in the air, and his voice is abruptly turned off. He's so startled that he can only sit down and glower out the door of his cell.

They bring him food and water, but otherwise ignore him.

After a restless night when he chooses to sleep on the floor rather than the lumpy sleeping pallet, Caden hears the Captain of the Guard approaching, conversing with Kairon.

"Lord Kairon, I must insist on your reassurance that he'll not cause any more trouble. We're far too busy to have to deal with a miscreant half-breed. Maybe you can find something for him to do." He looks Caden over. "He looks strong enough to do heavy carrying."

"Thank you, Attican, there will be no more incidents." He signals to Caden in the Rangers' sign language, to thank the captain but otherwise remain silent.

The captain traces a glamour that frees his voice. "Thank you Captain, I'm sorry for the trouble." He bites back his defence that he wasn't drinking.

"That was you on Cougar Mountain, wasn't it? With the Queen Designate." the Captain looks at him with stony eyes and says in the uncompromising voice of someone used to being obeyed, "I don't care who you're with. No more fighting or you'll be banished permanently from Queensdale."

He bows his head and follows Kairon from the stockade. Alone in the cell, he had time to consider the possible truth of what Kairon said to him, similar to the comments of the Venerable Dame. He hasn't been able to quell the bitterness, but he keeps his thoughts to himself.

Kairon doesn't speak to him, and doesn't try to hide his anger as he strides down the long hallways, his scabbard making a slight tapping noise as it bounces against his leg. He leads Caden to a far corner of the palace, to offices tucked in one of the oldest towers. He has a quiet conversation with an official, then turns stiffly to his son. “Lord Damian is the assistant Herald. He supervises and trains messengers. He’s a trusted ally. He’ll give you duties to keep you occupied. You will follow his instructions without question.”

Servants bring out a uniform with a visored cap, and Kairon hands them to Caden. “This uniform will give you access to most of the palace. Courtiers and servants will generally ignore you. Keep your ears open, keep the cap on to avoid eye contact, guard your tongue, and report back to me every day.” His stern voice softens for a moment. “I'm sorry our first true meeting was so difficult. But regardless of your feelings for me, our first priority is to protect Sislie and get her safely to the Grand Conclave.”

Caden bites back the explanation that leaps to his mouth. “Yes, sir.” He nods to his father and turns to follow Damian to his new messenger quarters.

CHAPTER 41

Kairon comes to teach me every day. The ceremonies, the speeches, the responses, the dedications. I've memorized almost all of them, but it's hard. I'm good at memorizing long and complex dance routines, but all these speeches make my head hurt.

On the fourth day of the Grand Conclave, I will be anointed by the priestesses who guard the grotto of the god TAN. Then I'll be Queen of the Fae. Queen Sislie. It sounds so wrong. I still keep thinking about Marielle, and what a good and skillful Queen she would have been, and how the Fae will have to put up with me, a poor substitute.

Kairon continues with lessons about court life and the current state of the Clans and Queendom. The lineages are complex and endless, the rivalries and alliances shift around like blowing leaves. The machinations of the court, and Lord Chamberlain Jarin's conspiracies, almost make me feel like when I was drugged and my brain felt like it was stuffed with feathers. I don't understand why they can't just get along. I have a good memory and my mother's clover tea to help keep my thinking clear, but where will I find the wisdom to sort through this quagmire?

Liana brings me untainted food every day, with tasty greetings from Gundega in the kitchen.

Two days before conclave, Liana hurries in bringing an ancient scroll from the royal quarters. We pore over it, but can't decipher the glyphs.

Later, the Venerable Ylva comes for my last lesson on the rites of anointing. She tells me the priestesses of the pool where I'm to receive the elixir will bestow some kind of awakening, but she's been vague about it, so I'm not sure what it entails.

She notices the scroll on a side table and takes it in her parchment hands. She peers intently at the glyphs. "This is one of four scrolls only the Queen should know about. How do you have it?"

"Liana has a spyhole behind the royal bedchamber. The Queen takes these scrolls out every day and examines them. She dropped this one the floor when she was putting them away, and it rolled under her bed."

"I saw these when Maelys was first Queen, when we were close friends. I wonder if they will explain her obsession with the supposed dragons." She traces a complex Revealing spell over the parchment and the glyphs seem to rise up from the vellum and become larger. "Your anointing ritual will give you the ability to read them, but I might be able to decipher some of it."

Her finger moves quickly from one glyph to the next, but she shakes her head. "There's much here I don't understand, but this is the symbol for the Land, this one for Mountain, and this for Healing. Further down, I'm pretty sure this one is Dragon, and this one is Blood, right beside it. Then the Healing glyph again. I'm sorry I can't give you more, but soon you'll be able to read it yourself."

She pats the settee beside her and I sit down next to her. She takes my hands in hers and looks at me with her clear gaze. "Sislie, you have everything you need to become Queen. You are honest and courageous, and your heartfire is strong. That's the most important thing. When you receive the elixir, trust it to show you what to do. You will heal the land. Everything else follows."

I always feel heartened by the Venerable Dame, and again I feel myself growing inside. Even when she doesn't say anything, her glowing presence gives me confidence. All this time I've kept thinking I won't be as good as Marielle, but she's finally convinced me that I don't have to be like Marielle. I just have to be the Queen that I'll be. It'll be different, but that doesn't mean worse. And with the support of my good helpers and advisors, I'll be as good a Queen as I can be.

What would I do without Liana and Kairon? She's agreed to stay on after I become Queen, and every day I'm more impressed at how she and Kairon manage to keep the Queendom functioning in spite of Maelys.

The Queen's tantrums and shrieking tirades are a daily occurrence now and she's absent from almost all court functions and meetings. She cares only about capturing the dragons, and, strangely, the final ball at the end of the Grand Conclave. Even though she's supposed to be teaching me to be Queen, I'm glad she mostly ignores me.

But near the end of the day, she summons me to her drawing room. When I arrive, Lord Jarin is just leaving. He bows and gives me his usual unctuous smile, but avoids my eyes.

She keeps me standing in front of her opulent settee. "Young Sislie." I hate her stinging voice and the way she looks at me like a predator savoring her next meal. "It's very important that you follow all of my instructions exactly when we get to the pool." She traces a Compliance spell in the air between us, not noticing that I deflect it. "That's all that matters—you must obey me." She mumbles about making sure I eat all my meals, and something about dragons that I can't make out. Then she talks about her only love who betrayed her, and gives me a strange look. "You'll never suffer such a loss, as I did."

What was supposed to be a lesson just leaves me with more questions. But I don't ask her anything lest I provoke another tantrum. I bow as soon as she seems to be finished muttering, and hurriedly take my leave. Liana is waiting for me, and takes me back to my rooms. She confirms the story about the Queen's heartbreak, but is just as confused as I am about the comment that I'll never suffer the same loss.

At the end of day, after everyone's gone, I'm all alone, with only Spark to keep me company. I've gotten used to the luxurious quarters with their brilliant hangings and splendid furnishings, and I'm even getting used to being waited on for everything. But I hate the isolation. I feel more like a prisoner than the royal trainee. Even with the Venerable Dame's reassurance, the doubts creep in again. I'm scared of what I have to become, that I won't be up to the task. And I'm still resentful that I'm in this position. I should be able to get over it, but I can't, in spite of knowing how crucial it is to the Queendom.

I miss Caden, and I'm worried about him. I haven't seen him since he stormed out of my room after learning about Kairon. I wonder where he is, and what he's doing.

My stretching routine gives me comfort. I use the back of the elegant settee as a barre to stretch out my calves and hamstrings, then twist and press my arms upward and down to ease my back, which has been stiff from sitting too much. I envision my ensemble of dancers as I do a few simple arabesques, extending my leg behind me and leaning forward as I curve my arms high. I imagine musicians and the bright wisps of light swirling around us.

A soft thump interrupts my preparation to do a small leap and *flicker*, and Caden appears at the doorway to my sleeping chamber. I rush into his arms. "Where have you been?"

He holds me first, then kisses me, long and deep. He doesn't let go for a good long time. My fear and worries dissipate as though he were the healer, and I the wounded one.

"Kairon has me running errands for the assistant Herald. See my apprentice messenger uniform?" He steps away and does a little sashay around me in his peaked cap and short grey cape, making me laugh for the first time since our night together.

"I've learned my way around the palace, including more of the hidden passages. This uniform is almost as good as an Unnoticeable spell, because everyone ignores me. So I get to go almost everywhere, and I've seen a lot. I report to Kairon every day."

"How are things between you and your father?"

"I've been so used to hating him all these years, it's hard to accept what both he and the Venerable Dame said about the role he played in my life. But we've both been very busy and haven't talked about it." He presses his lips together and frowns slightly, but then shrugs his shoulders. "I don't know if I'll ever like him, but I can see that he's very capable. He has quite an alliance among the courtiers, Guards and servants. They work hard to keep the Queendom safe until the next Queen is anointed." He gives me a cheeky grin and a little bow. "That's you. What can I do for you, your almost Majesty?"

I take him by the hand and walk him to my bed, smiling. "You can do that thing that makes me arch my back, but really slowly." He throws off his messenger's cape with a sly grin. We explore new pleasures until the dawn sends its first golden ribbon through the high window in my chamber. I fall asleep in his comforting arms, the only place I feel really safe in this palace, full of spies and schemers.

The next morning Caden is still in my sleeping chamber when my parents come for their consultation with Kairon.

Nerysa quickly hides her annoyance when she sees him there, and Torin purses his lips and looks away. The Fae are usually casual about romantic and sexual liaisons, so I'm surprised to see them react this way.

Liana comes to supplement my tainted breakfast with good food from Gundega. My mother inspects the food, then checks me over again, noting that there are no signs of unwanted glamours or medicines. Kairon takes Caden's account from the previous day, and sends him to report for messenger duty.

Gundega comes in through the same passage Caden uses, to give her report. In the kitchen, she has quickly become a valuable informant for Kairon and Liana's network. Housekeepers and servants speak freely around the broken Fae, beneath their notice, with her gruff manner and apparent indifference to those around her.

After Gundega returns, Kairon and my parents share their latest information on Jarin and his faction.

Then Kairon confers with all of us about the court, who can be trusted, and what is likely to happen after the Grand Conclave. After I return from the Grotto and leave for Dragon's End, they'll have to move fast to displace Jarin and return the Royal treasury so Jarin can't use it to fund his aspirations.

Liana, Kairon and Torin go to collect the overnight report from their spy network. Nerysa stays behind.

As soon as they're out the door, she astonishes me. "Sislie, your friendship with young Caden is not appropriate. He spends too much time in your quarters, and there is talk in the corridors that you have taken a halfbreed lover."

"How is this your business, mother?" I burst out, shocked that she'd criticize me about something like this. "You've never interfered with my friendships before, and now is not a good time to start."

"This seems to be much more than a friendship, my dear. Didn't Caden sleep here last night?"

"If he did, it's still none of your business. You know I hate this life, and I'm fully aware that no Queen has ever taken a half-Human as Royal Consort." All my fear and anxiety pour out onto my mother. "But what's it to anyone if I have a loving companion who comforts me in this wretched place?"

"Darling Sislie, it's all different now, you know that. The palace is full of gossip and intrigue. I don't want you to start your royal duties under the taint of scandal."

"Mind your own business, mother." My frustration boils over and I shout. "I never wanted this in the first place. I'm not the perfect Marielle, I'm just muddling through the best I can. If that's not good enough, too bad. I don't need you treating me like a child and undermining my confidence." I stomp into my sleeping quarters, firmly closing the door behind me. I'm so mad, what do they expect from me? I feel like throwing things and pounding on the walls of this luxurious prison.

I stop and look at the bed, still rumpled from last night. The memory of pleasure diverts me from my anger at my mother, and my body remembers the reassurance and comfort he gave me last night. I start my breathing routine, which always worked to help me stay focused for a performance. *Breathe in. Hold. Breathe out. Hold. Breath in. Hold. Breathe out. Breathe.* The angry thoughts dissipate, and I start to stretch and sway in rhythm as I chant, *I can do this, I know I can do this, I can do this, I know I can do this.*

CHAPTER 42

Caden lounges against the wall beside the door to Jarin's study, casually studying a piece of paper in his hand, as though considering his next errand.

"Uncle, you promised it would be taken care of." Lady Tyra's voice rises in a whine. She has long black hair and her pale violet eyes are like Jarin's. She wears a sapphire blue silken gown, more laden with jewels than an ordinary day in the palace would call for. Her ostentatious headpiece looks suspiciously like a crown, rather than what a Lady in waiting would wear. Her long face is made even longer by her pout. "She was never supposed to..."

"You mustn't be overeager, my dear. Our Heron clan will produce another Queen Designate if required, but you must be patient. She's here now. Leave it to me." His condescending voice fails to pacify her, and she doesn't notice his frown as she continues to pace back and forth in front of his desk. "We still have a few days before the Grand Conclave, and I'm confident Her Majesty is on your side."

Caden presses himself to the wall as Lady Tyra storms out of her uncle's study, then hurries down the passage toward Kairon's study.

CHAPTER 43

The Queen storms around her bedchamber, raging, smashing precious ornaments from her dressing table onto the floor. "Surely it can't be so difficult to capture one half-grown dragon. Incompetents! Just because they can fly is no excuse."

Maelys unravels the scroll again and pores over it, once more examining the reference to dragon blood and its power. She takes a deep breath, and her fervid imagination presents her with marvellous pictures of herself, young again, full of life, sparkling, dancing at the ball, laughing, pursued by endless suitors. She renews her Youthfulness glamour and preens in front of the ornately carved and bejewelled mirror standing on the floor near her dressing room, displeasure forgotten, her mouth practicing a charming smile.

There's a quiet knock at the door, and the thirteen priestesses of the Grotto push their way in, sweeping past the protestations of the handmaidens who have been waiting in the drawing room to help the Queen out of her gown and into her nightdress.

"What do you want? Get out of here!" All traces of charm vanished, she hastily tucks the scroll under an embroidered cushion. "Can't you see I'm busy?"

"Your Majesty, we are here to help you prepare for your upcoming visit to the Grotto, and your sacred union with the god TAN." The priestesses slowly form a circle around the old Queen, quietly humming. "We bring healing meditations, and a calming tisane to help you make ready for this ultimate act of your reign."

"I don't need any preparation. Get out!"

"Majesty…"

"Get out, get out, get out!" her shrieking makes the handmaidens in the next room cringe and cover their ears. "And take your meditations with you. And your medications too. Get out!"

The senior priestess frowns and exchanges glances with her sisters. After a long moment, she nods and they stop humming. They slowly trail out behind her, casting worried looks over their shoulders. She tells the handmaidens to attend to their Queen.

The handmaidens hurry in with a nightdress. She has already pulled off her headpiece, and tossed it on the floor. As usual, she scolds the young females for being clumsy. While they remove her gown, she mutters under her breath about dragons, about blood. The nervous handmaidens finish helping her get ready for bed and scuttle away as quickly as they can.

The old Queen tucks the scroll back into its cupboard, then opens a tiny drawer hidden in the ornate carving at the back of her dresser. She takes out a small plain looking dagger with an ebony handle, and a tiny blue glass vial with a cork stopper. She removes the dagger from its nondescript leather sheath and opens the vial. She brings it to her nose and takes a sniff, then dribbles several drops of the blue liquid on the blade of the knife. She mutters to herself, "That will do it. Stupid little dancer—how dare she think she can take my place!" This time there is no charm to her smile.

CHAPTER 44

I wake up hungry. It's supposed to be my big day, but I'm just hungry. And cranky. And anxious, even though I'm snuggled in Caden's reassuring arms. He's been by my side every night since he overheard Jarin and his niece plotting against me. But I'm so tired of all the fuss and subterfuge, I almost look forward to being Queen, just to get it over with.

A gentle knock at the door announces Liana with three simpering ladies-in-waiting, bearing an enormous bundle of dazzling pink gown and an overflowing armload of fluffy silver feathers. Servants process in after them with a tray of savory breakfast tarts, raspberries and cherries that, as usual, give off a faint trace of taint. Liana slips a small bundle under my bedclothes.

The ladies start to fuss and lay out the elaborate gown and train I'm to wear today. The pile of silver feathers turns out to be the headdress. Liana shoos them out the door, saying I have to meditate, then break my fast before they come back to dress me. She takes the platter and messes up the food, then takes a large serving and throws it down the privy. I gobble some uncontaminated fruit and the nut bread she brought, and drink water from her small flask.

Too soon, the ladies-in-waiting are knocking at the door again to dress me for the procession. The pink gown is made of the same gossamer silk I'd wear as a dancer, but there are too many layers, all weighed down with jewels on golden strands—emeralds, rubies, diamonds, moonstones, aquamarines—each representing one of the Fae clans that I am to serve, or rule over, or whatever. It's the first day of Grand Conclave, and my debut appearance before the Clans.

Now I'm not cranky any more, just nervous. I have all the speeches and dedications memorized. I'm not worried about that, but I still can't shake off the feeling that I'm an impostor.

Caden slipped away when the ladies came for me, but his presence still thrums at the edges of my awareness. But where's Gundega? She's supposed to be in the procession and I need her gruff and reassuring presence.

Finally, the gown is positioned to the satisfaction of the ladies-in-waiting. Its billowing layers hide my feet, encased in velvet slippers bearing even more jewels. As they finish fastening the absurd feathered headdress, pulling my curly hair impossibly tight into the cap that holds it, there's another knock on the door to announce Kairon and the courtiers who will accompany me to the first day of Grand Conclave. I feel like a stuffed doll that should be displayed on someone's dresser, not like a capable and intelligent candidate for Queen. But I follow them out, stepping as tall and lightly as I can.

Kairon walks beside me, then the lords and ladies of the court, and behind them is Gundega, still limping slightly, dressed in a blue silken gown like one of the ladies. I can't help but giggle when I see her. It's the first time I've seen her wearing anything but burlap. She looks dour as always, visibly uncomfortable in the finery, but her eyes brighten as she glances my way, smiles and winks. Her face is determined and protective, and I feel reassured by her presence.

We process down a wide walkway of arched trees, coaxed to form an enclosed path. My gown is almost as wide as the path, its many layers keeping anyone from coming too close.

When we emerge at the edge of the dale, Kairon leaves me to stand escort to Queen Maelys, who has just arrived on her palanquin.

I'm alone at the head of the procession. I take a few steps forward and blink at the transformed dale. It was all covered in gray ash when we arrived at Queensdale, but now it looks like a glittering field of brilliantly colored flowers. As I draw closer, the colors and shapes resolve into clusters of Fae. So many Fae. I knew all the clans would be represented, but in such numbers? Is this every Fae from every clan? All looking at me with love and expectation, trusting I will heal the land, mediate their disputes, do something about the Raiders. Gods!

Our path curves down the side of the vale to a silken pavilion with striped poles supporting a brocade awning. Beneath it the queen sits tiny and silent on one of a pair of carved wooden thrones, each one suggesting a peacock with thirteen tail feathers, one for each clan. She's almost hidden beneath her own elaborate headdress.

We approach from behind, but as we round the corner and arrive at the front of the pavilion, a ripple of silence spreads through the throng and all the Fae, courtiers and entertainers fall to their knees. Even my parents and little cousin Cathrie, at the front of the gathered Clans. I stop and stand as tall as I can. I try to accept this homage. I've always enjoyed the enthusiasm of our dance audiences, but this is beyond compare, overwhelming. I remember to take a deep breath.

The old Queen waves her hand at me to join her on the other throne.

Kairon's powerful voice carries across the dale. "Welcome your new Queen."

A mighty roar and cheer erupts from the gathered Clans. The sky explodes in dancing colors and fountains of hummingbirds. After a while, the illusion settles into a serene landscape surrounding a replica of Queensdale palace. Then the music starts up again, and jugglers, dancers, and acrobats join a parade that stretches around the spacious clearing.

Thirteen towering banners proclaim the Clans. First is the Falcon banner, displaying the great predators plummeting down a steep and craggy slope. The Queen's Clan. Followed by the rest, each grander than the one before. And at the end, my Hummingbird Clan—its banner displaying the familiar tiny birds darting endlessly among brilliant red and yellow flowers.

I always thought the Grand Conclave would be a solemn occasion, but this is delightful, a cacophony of joy, more like a festival. Jugglers with iridescent orbs circulate among stilt walkers emulating the giants and gods of old. There are amazing creatures coaxed by the Lynx Clan into impossible but glorious combinations of feather and fur, claw and horn—long necked creatures with heads that look like great bouquets of will-o'-the-wisp, giant pea-cats with brilliant aquamarine heads and tail feathers sparkling silver and blue, centurions with the lower bodies of horses and the chest and arms of lordly looking monkeys.

And the music—it's as though all the music of all the clans has been woven into textures that bathe my skin, and melodies that dance with each other and make me forget, for a moment, what this is. And the dancers. I want to swirl down to join them.

But I remember with a jolt I'll never again be one of them.

At another time, I would have feasted and celebrated all night with my cousins and fellow dancers. But not now. Before the afternoon is over, Queen Maelys returns to the palace on her palanquin. She hasn't said a word all day, mostly watching the sky, occasionally sipping her hibiscus mead and muttering something I can't hear.

I follow soon after, brushing off the offer to be carried on my own palanquin. I'm desperate for the short walk after having to sit for so long, smiling and applauding all the performances, each one more fabulous and ingenious than the one before. I would have enjoyed them more if my head didn't hurt from having my hair pulled tight under the ridiculous headdress.

Back in my rooms, the ladies divest me of the finery, and servants bring more tainted food, refreshments for the evening. I send everyone away, then do my stretches and warmups to move my body around after the long hours of inactivity.

First thing in the morning, the tittering incursion of handmaidens arrives with yet another extravagant gown and headdress for the second day. I do my best to put up with it, but I can't help feeling they're like coaxers, trying to make me into something I'm not.

The procession and acclaim are much like yesterday, but today starts the formal meeting of each of the Clans.

First comes the presentation by the outgoing Queen's Falcon Clan. Graceful youth approach, bearing great platters of food. Gundega's reassuring nod gives me permission to eat. I haven't had anything yet, but as Liana bends to place a small table in front of me, she whispers a reminder, "Just a tiny nibble. There will be many of these today and you have to take from each one."

I'm hungry, but I only take a couple of tiny bites from each platter, daintily as I can, resisting my impulse to gobble. Tiny cakes and flans made with berries and nuts, ingenious melon figures shaped like birds and flowers, each a delight to see, smell and taste. Delicate berry wines, mead from the best of their beekeepers. After I take a taste, each platter is circulated among the rest of the clans, feeding everyone, symbolizing sharing and trust.

Then the gifts. First, they bow to Maelys, the outgoing Queen, and declaim in the most florid language, thanking her for her centuries of dedicated service. They recount tales of her wise and courageous rule and healing powers, and wish her serenity and contentment as she accepts her new role. They present her with a feather that winks in and out of sight, a token of their Clan.

Maelys sits through the presentation, thin lips in a straight line, nodding briefly in acknowledgement. All the stories of her wisdom and courage are from long ago. I wonder what she's thinking, so close to the end of her reign, and her life as she knows it. As they finish, she glances at me with a strange glitter in her eye that makes my skin crawl.

Then it's my turn. Clan elders come forward, followed by youth and children carrying gifts. Sumptuous fabrics, jewels in elven-crafted caskets with cunning puzzle fastenings made to look like decoration, a plain looking bow and quiver of arrows, which I'm sure will be inscribed with enchanted runes. At the end, they present me with an ornately embroidered red and gold banner depicting the sigils of Falcon and Hummingbird intertwined, to symbolize the friendship between our Clans.

After the presentation of gifts, the ritual promise. "We of the Falcon clan dedicate our allegiance to the Queen. To help and serve, to follow wise council, to keep the clans united and safe, and to protect the Land."

Then I speak the ritual words. "I, Sislie, of the Hummingbird Clan, accept your fealty and promise to be your Queen. To serve the Clans, the Land, and all who dwell within, with justice and mercy, and without favor. This I covenant, with all that I do, all that I am, and all that I have."

After that, their performance. The Falcon Clan are wondrous archers. Beautiful young Fae, both male and female, form into a circle, drawing their bows. They fire magic crafted arrows in a stunning display of mock battles and brightly coloured cascades. This evokes many cheers and sparkling lights flung in the air, which is how the Fae show their appreciation. Then all of the arrows speed back to their owners and tuck neatly back into the quivers they came in.

I'm amazed. For a moment, I even forget that it's all for me. But there will be thirteen of these, for each of the thirteen Clans. Squirrel, Lynx, Beaver, Otter, Cougar, Heron, Wolf, Owl, Deer, Fox, Raven, and last will be my own Hummingbird Clan. It'll take two days.

Each Clan's presentation and dedication follows the same pattern. First the feast, then the gift to Queen Maelys, each giving her a grand speech and a token of their clan—an acorn, a golden light, a bead, a carved twig—symbolic gifts for one who will not be long with us. Then more gifts for me, the promises, and finally, the performance.

By the end of the second day, I'm exhausted. I'm overloaded with food and sumptuousness, and more attention than I can bear. I've had to be fully aware and focused on each presentation of gifts and dedications. My only respite was during the concluding performances of each Clan, and when the presentations were being made to the outgoing Queen.

My eyes are tired of looking interested yet serene, as I was coached, and my throat aches from declaiming loudly enough to be heard across the dale. I want to be done. I want to curl up and rest in Caden's arms. I thought I caught a glimpse of him a couple of times, but apprentice messengers and other unimportant household servants are gathered too far back for me to get a good look.

Maelys has been strangely silent throughout this process. Other than a bit of muttering, she hasn't said a word, not even scolding and complaining the way she usually does.

Though oddly, when one of the coaxer clans displays a couple of giant lizards induced to develop wings, she jolts out of an apparent doze and starts to get up out of her peacock throne, shouting something I can't make out. Kairon steps in front of her and bends down to whisper in her ear. After a few moments, she settles back down and reaches for her cup of hibiscus mead.

On the third day, the presentations continue.

Then it's time for the last Clan. The Hummingbird Clan. My parents are not part of the presentations, but they stand proudly smiling at me from the front of the throng. I look around for Caden but I can't spot him.

I'm delighted to see the glowing dancers twirl and *flicker* in the familiar and beloved choreography, billowing wings swirling together with the folds of their silken costumes. My fellow dancers, my cousins. I've spent all of my life with them. I anticipate every move they make. Musicians with flutes, bells, and hand drums encircle and weave among them as they approach, wreathed in clouds of wisps coaxed into my favorite turquoise.

I want to laugh, then I want to cry. I want to leap out of my chair, stupid throne. I should have been one of them. Wing nubs humming, my feet start to tap out the familiar steps. Until I feel Kairon's steady and gentle hand on my shoulder, quenching my impulse. "You must receive their gift graciously, not try to be one of them."

The youth bearing platters of food are my cousins and friends. I've missed their familiar faces. I want to leap up and hug them and jump around like when we were children, but instead I hold back and do my best to maintain a gracious smile. The chefs have outdone themselves, knowing how much I love food. They've brought my favorite delicacies, forming pastries into tiny castles and delicate fruit ices in the shape of dancers. Even the brambleberry wine that was my occasional downfall is presented in an exquisite crystal flute formed to look like the healer's flame in the center of my hummingbird sigil.

I'm overwhelmed with the love my Clan is showing, but I don't deserve it. Trying not to cry, I choke down a few small delicacies, and a tiny sip of the wine.

Somehow, I get through the gifts and dedications, my voice wooden. I want to confess that I'm not worthy of their love, that I'm guilty I caused so much trouble, that I'm sorry I'm not Marielle. I should be filled with joy, but I can't feel it. I can't appreciate the cunning and luxurious elven-crafted gifts or the rare and precious healing herbs they present to me.

The delegation masks their disappointment at my lack of enthusiasm as I declaim in a subdued voice, clenching my jaw to keep from sobbing.

I watch their marvellous final performance with a leaden heart. I'll never dance with them again. Never experience that electrifying moment of time stopped as we *flicker* in and out of view. Never feel the delicious touch of fingertip and glance as we arabesque in star formation, or the feather light grazing of wing tips as we form a circle back-to-back and *flicker* out of sight only to meet again in the center, throwing out a glorious cascade of golden lights. Never again.

I always knew I was next in line in case Marielle was unable to be Queen, but that was just a formality. Never in the history of the Fae has this ever been. We always took it for granted that she'd be the Queen and I the dancer. I feel like an impostor having the Fae I grew up with bowing to me.

At last, the third day is over. I'm so exhausted I even let them carry me back to my rooms on a palanquin. It's a weird bumpy ride with four Queen's Guards walking in step, each bearing one end of the two poles that hold up the chair, and I feel a bit foolish, knowing how easily I could get there on my own. But I'm grateful for the ride. They settle me down with great care outside my quarters, where Liana and the fluttering ladies are already waiting for me.

After they wrestle off my gown and headpiece, Liana brings me my nightgown and sends them all away. She leaves me with another flask of spring water, then takes her leave as well. I'm too restless to sleep, so I try a few token stretches, but end up flopping into one of the soft chairs. The voices of the clans are still echoing in my ears, and eventually I fall asleep sprawled out on the chair.

Sometime during the night, strong arms lift me and carry me to my bed. I nuzzle into the refuge of his clean, manly smell, and feel his kisses on my face. He holds me for a time but leaves before dawn, and I drift into a dreamless sleep.

CHAPTER 45

In the morning, the Venerable Ylva is sitting in the chair I fell asleep in. Her soft smile is a benediction. Her deep luminous gaze recognizes the me I discovered at her chalet. She raises both hands with her open palms facing me, and I feel a cleansing breeze waft through me.

By the time I'm fully awake, she's gone. I'm not sure if she was really there or I only dreamed her. But for once I'm free of the doubts that have plagued me this whole time. I know I'll always miss dancing, but I remember my resolve, and who I am to be. Filled with new confidence, I review my memorized speeches for the day of anointing.

The ladies process into my rooms bearing a heavy ceremonial robe, embroidered with Clan symbols, the elementals—elves, naiads, dryads and merfolk—and historical figures like dragons, dwarves, giants and gods. The robe has a slight lustre, like the tapestries in the Queen's and Venerable Dame's chambers. It goes over a plain crimson gown, the same color as my sigil's heartfire. The ladies are miffed when I refuse their offer to tame my hair with braids and coil it neatly around my head, but for once, they don't try to insist. I've always preferred to let it go free, and today I don't want a headache from their pulling and twisting.

When the procession arrives at the dale, the clans are quiet, kneeling silently until Kairon invites them to rise. Queen Maelys again sits silent on her dais, eyes almost closed, her mouth a thin line behind her Youthfulness glamour.

This morning is the oaths of fealty. First the Clan leaders, binding them to me and to one another. Pledges to protect the Land, give aid to one another and live in peace. This time I watch them, making note for later of who is sincere, and who is less than enthusiastic.

Then officials of the court, swearing their loyalty. Jarin is first. I'm barely able to hide my revulsion as his slimy voice speaks words he doesn't mean. The remaining courtiers follow, one by one, declaiming their oaths. The palace has been in chaos for so long that Jarin's coterie can't hide their duplicity behind thinly disguised smirks. I'm grateful for Kairon, steadfast behind me, and I wonder how we'll manage to dislodge them from their powerful positions. I stoutly refuse the despair that threatens to creep in and undermine my courage. I can *flicker*. I can heal. I have faced a forest fire. I have saved a dragon. I can do this.

After a simple midday meal, the thirteen Guardians of the Grotto approach the pavilion, dressed in plain hooded robes the color of pale moss. The youngest one carries a wreath of woven birch twigs. These are the priestesses dedicated to guarding the sleeping place of the god TAN, where I'm to receive the elixir tomorrow. Two of them take my robe, holding it aloft.

The eldest of the priestesses bids me unfurl my wings and extend them to their fullest, to receive the quintessential energy of the Aether, the cosmic energy. I hadn't known this would be part of the ritual, but I release them from my wing nubs. As I stretch them out, a tight smallness in me lets go too, and I breathe in deeply. I'm ready.

The priestesses raise their hands with palms facing me for the final rite of anointing. As I begin to say the memorized dedication, my heartfire surges throughout my body, and the words buzz out of my mouth in the ancient tongue. *"I hear the need. I heed the summons. I will heal the land."*

The words bind me to the Land, to the Clans, to protect and heal the Humans who share the land, the elves, naiads, and dryads, and the merfolk who inhabit our shores. To give our aid and save them from any who would do them harm. And to Dragon's End Mountain, where the poison emanates, at whose core perished the dragons who gave us life.

As I speak the ancient words, I feel like I'm growing taller. With each breath, I'm filled with strength, courage, even joy. The doubts might still be there, but I know I have the resources to be a good and capable Queen. I have my family and my helpers, but mostly, something inside me expands as I take on this new persona. I am the Queen. I am the one who'll heal the land. All else can be learned. I feel the long line of Queens speaking through me, dedicated to the same task.

The youngest priestess approaches me and places the now luminous circlet of woven birch on my head. They all chant in the same buzzing tongue that came out of my mouth during the dedications. Their words open a locked compartment in my mind, and I now understand the ancient tongue. Also, the unexpected final instruction they give me. Then they bow silently and fade away from the platform.

My first duty as Queen of the Fae, after I drink the elixir, will be to climb to the top of Dragon's End Mountain. I already knew this. But the last invocation of the priestesses told me that when I get to the top of the mountain, I am to fill the cup with my blood, to share my own essence, now infused with the power of the god who sleeps in the pool. Then I'm to pour it on the highest point of the mountain.

It's my blood that will start to neutralize the toxins and heal the mountain. I shiver nervously. I've never seen the cup. I hope it's not very big.

After the priestesses leave, I turn to face the Clans, my Clans. I look out over the colorful field, seeing everyone with new eyes, the eyes of a Queen. I can see the hope, the trust, and also the greed and scheming. Kairon steps forward and loudly hails Queen Sislie. The whole dale kneels. It's a solemn occasion, but I can't help but grin when they all leap to their feet and I hear the roars of acclamation and see the air filled with sparkling lights.

I am the Queen. But for this day, there are two Queens. I take a quick glance at Maelys, who still sits silent and unmoving on her throne, eyes veiled, mouth a thin line. I wonder what she's feeling. Is she relieved to be free of her burden? Anticipating ecstasy at merging with the god? Merely resigned to her fate? Her face shows nothing.

An uneasy shiver flutters down my spine.

CHAPTER 46

One last speech. I step forward to call out the ritual question to the Clans. But as I open my mouth to speak the words, I'm interrupted by a loud roar and the flapping of enormous wings. A magnificent turquoise and silver dragon hurtles out of the sky and plunges to land on the ground in front of the pavilion, scattering everyone from the center of the clearing. It's the female, the larger of the two dragons we encountered on Cougar Mountain. There's a tall, skinny youth, with something of a Fae look about him, riding her neck on some kind of saddle. As he starts to slide off, another dragon lands beside her. It's Fancy. Who Caden and I rescued.

I bow deeply to the dragons, as do the silent Clans.

Everyone stares, transfixed, as the young man dismounts his dragon and walks towards the pavilion, holding out his hand. There's something round and turquoise resting on the palm of his hand. He bows and reaches it up to me shyly, "It's a dragon scale from Fancy, your Majesty, a token of his thanks."

I'm deeply honored to receive such a gift, and again bow to Fancy, who takes a step closer to the dais, looking at me with his swirling golden eyes. My mind is filled with a picture of flying with him to the top of a smoking mountain. He comes closer and extends a long, leathery wing toward me.

He's inviting me to fly! I take a step toward him, bowing again, heart pounding, desperately wanting to take up his offer. But I apologize as best I can, and humbly explain that I'm not ready to go to the top of the mountain. That will be tomorrow. I feel a trace of amusement from him, and hear a sound in my head as he withdraws his wing. He nods to me. <<*SSSISSSLEE*>>

He turns to the other dragon as the lad scampers back up her wing to his saddle. But just then, Queen Maelys, who has been watching in stunned silence along with everyone else, suddenly leaps off her throne and starts running toward the dragons with a small knife in her hand, shrieking frantically to her Guards, "Take it, kill it, I need its blood!"

The whole conclave gasps at these words. A couple of the Guards reach for their bows, but their fellows slap them down. The Queen's handmaidens try to hold her back, but the tiny Fae gets an unexpected burst of strength and fights them off. She rushes toward the dragons, kicking off her jewelled slippers in her frenzy.

The dragons roar and send a small lick of fire in her direction, scorching the skirts of her gown. That doesn't stop her, but by then her Guards have reached her and they gently restrain the raving monarch. Maelys tries to fight them off, shrieking and crying for her dragon blood. Kairon orders her Guards and handmaidens to take her back to the palace. She continues trying to break away from them as they carry her on her palanquin, her screams echoing across the dale. The dragons launch into the air and fly off.

The Grand Conclave is in chaos, everyone babbling and shouting. As her shrill voice fades into the distance, Kairon raises his hands and calls for quiet in his powerful voice. The babbling subsides. He looks at me and steps aside.

After the final speeches and dedication, I was supposed to call out the ritual question: What can we do for the clans? I look out over the dale, full of expectant faces. At last I can see Caden, who has worked his way close to the front, standing next to Gundega and my parents. He's grinning at me the same way he did when we freed Fancy that night on the mountain. I step forward. Now I know what to say.

"Thank you for welcoming me as your new Queen in these extraordinary circumstances," I call out, my voice clear and confident. "This is the beginning of my reign, but more importantly, it's the beginning of a new age. There have been no dragons since the time before remembering, but now they have returned." The whole dale roars and cheers and fills the sky with sparkling lights. I wait for them to settle down, then continue, holding up the dragon scale for them to see.

"On my journey here with my companions, I had the honor and good fortune to make the acquaintance of Fancy, the dragon with the handsome silver ruff. I look forward to this being a long and happy friendship.

"But meanwhile, there's work to be done. I appoint Lord Kairon to be my senior advisor. He will help me as I begin my duties. Now I ask, what can we do for the clans?"

Someone calls out, "What about the Raiders who killed Marielle?"

I move aside as Kairon steps forward and answers on my behalf. He asks each Clan to keep their warriors in readiness, to defend the land. The Raiders have encroached on our side of the peninsula too many times, with dire results.

He requests that the elders of each Clan convene tomorrow, the last day of the Grand Conclave, to plan how to shore up our defenses and decide what's to be done about the Raiders. There are more questions and more requests. Some can be answered right away, others deferred until the Clan elders meet.

The ceremonies are over. There will be a farewell ball tonight in honor of Queen Maelys, though I'll not be in attendance, and I doubt she will be there either. The Clans will soon return home except for the youth who will stay behind to serve their rotation for the new Queen. Jarin and some courtiers try to insist that I be carried on my palanquin, but Kairon shoos them away, saying I should return as I wish.

Liana has agreed to stay on and serve the new Queen. She walks behind me and Kairon, then Gundega, followed by the handmaidens who will remain, and the youth who will be my new servers.

The incomprehensible outburst of the old Queen has left me perplexed and uneasy, and her frantic shrieks still echo in my brain as we process off the platform and back up the path to my new home.

CHAPTER 47

We return to the palace, through the walkway that I hardly see this time. I can't really take it in. I felt joy and love during the dedication, and my mind is still reeling at the sudden arrival of the dragons. But now I'm just limp. And anxious. I'm suddenly responsible for so many things. I have to save the land from poison, and my court is riddled with corrupt courtiers holding secrets I'm not privy to.

I can see my parents watching me from the edge of the walkway. My mother stands tall and proud beside my father, both of them giving me that look that says, 'I know you can do this,' just like when I was a little dancer getting ready for my first performance. Their confidence takes the edge off my anxiety, just as it did then. I look back at them with hope and gratitude in my heart.

We process up the walkway. Queen Maelys is no doubt back in her quarters. I'm worried about her outburst. What does she want with the dragons? Blood? Is it just madness? The dragon scale from Fancy is still in my hand, and I rub it with my thumb. I wonder if there's something in those ancient scrolls. I wonder what this final night will be for her.

When we arrive, Liana, the ladies-in-waiting, and several other handmaidens are waiting for me. They guide me to a new section of the palace I've never seen before. The coaxers have been growing this suite for the Queen-to-be for many years, since long before I was born. My new rooms are elegant and beautiful, thankfully not overly ornate. The walls are covered with luminous tapestries, one of them depicting a circle of dancers from my Clan. Clusters of will-o'-the-wisp form chandeliers lighting each room in warm glowing light. The furnishings all look either coaxed or elven-crafted, and even in my tired state, I stop to admire them.

Delicate silken coverlets are heaped on a bed that only the best of master coaxers could have shaped, inviting and warm.

The handmaidens help me out of the heavy ceremonial robes, which they take away, leaving me with Liana. She helps me into my nightgown and dims the wisps, tucking me into bed as though I were her sister, not the queen.

"Tomorrow I'll come with you to the entrance of the grotto, but after that it'll be just you and Queen Maelys, and one attendant. Gundega will go with you."

I fall into a restless sleep. I dream of fire, and dragons, and grand spectacle. I dream of lying under a table, of being trapped in a tunnel. I dream of Caden, his arms, his laughing eyes. I dream of sinking into a dark pool, following the iridescence of a green stone as I swim into its deeps.

Gundega's gentle shake wakes me. The wisps hover in a subdued glow, the deep night gives no hint of dawn at the window. "It's time to go," she whispers. She helps me into a plain white shift, a simple gown and warm slippers, then wraps me into a comforting woolen cloak from Caden's mother.

The green stone from the dwarf tunnels is sitting on my bedside table. It's glowing again, just as it did in the deep pool when I found it. I pick it up and tuck it into a small pocket of my cloak.

This morning I fast, taking only a few sips of spring water before I go out.

A small procession is waiting for us at a side entrance to the palace. The Guardians of the Grotto, several of the Queen's attendants, my mother, and Liana all stand in silence as we join them. The Guardians' wings are unfurled, draping softly behind them, almost indistinguishable from their long white hair. The Queen arrives on her smallest palanquin, carried by four female warriors. Again inscrutable, she flicks her bony fingers that we should get going.

We traverse the edge of Queensdale valley by starlight, following a narrow trail that leads to the foot of Dragon's End Mountain. The white clad Guardians of the Pool lead the way, followed by Maelys, carried on her palanquin, until the Guardians gesture that her Guards can go no further.

We continue on foot, in silence. I walk with Gundega, Liana behind us, my mother and a few attendants following. I walk as though in a dream. The beauty of the night, the chilly air on my face, the soft tread of our feet, the rustling of small animals and night birds are all there, but I'm oblivious to them. It's like that moment in *flicker* when everything is suspended, except this moment is suspended indefinitely. I'm breathing so slowly that every so often my lungs shudder in a large gasp of air.

We arrive. We enter the mist that surrounds the grotto.

One of the pool elders reaches into a plain cloth pouch and takes something out of it, which she hands to Maelys. She tucks it into a pocket of her gown. The elders come to me and remove my cape and slippers and gown, until I'm shivering in the little shift that gives no warmth in the chilly mist. One of them gives these to Liana, then indicates that she and the others should withdraw from us.

The green stone is in my hand. It finds its way into a tiny pocket in my shift. There's still no hint of dawn.

CHAPTER 48

My bare foot steps cautiously into the mist. Then the other. One foot is all I can see below me. The mist obscures my vision and shrouds my ears with expectant stillness. Each step fades away as silently as the one before. The narrow path falls abruptly away beside me and slips away unseen behind. I touch the silken cord Gundega tied around my waist for safety. Through it I imagine I can feel her slight limp behind me. My other hand clutches the cord Queen Maelys holds as she leads the way. The faint shimmer of her simple gown is all I can see in front of me.

The silent anticipation and chilly air make me shiver. A nervous giggle dies in my throat. What if my destiny is to fall screaming off the edge of a cliff? But I hang on to the cord and follow quietly. The Guardians trail behind Gundega. They cautioned us to keep silent and we heed their admonition.

We follow her for a long time, stepping carefully to keep within the narrow edges of the path. It curves around, down the inside of a steep, narrow valley. I have lost all sense of direction, and time. I only know this is the day, and we're not there yet. I am ill prepared and nervous, but I'm ready to face what will come.

The path becomes wider. A pale luminescence insinuates itself into the fog and the outgoing Queen's gown ahead of me glimmers faintly green. Then the path feels different under my bare feet. Looking down, I see that we're walking on dilapidated bricks. The growing light reveals that we're on a ledge that continues to curve around the inside of the narrow valley. Eventually we step down into a tunnel—but not a tunnel, a walkway that looks out over the valley. I peer over the rail into a thinning mist.

Only it's not a valley. It's the remains of a vast structure, like an inverted castle lining the inside of an immense cone. What at first appeared to be the green of trees and bushes, is actually vines and moss covering most of the stonework. It's a breathtaking ruin—beautiful, elegant, majestic, enormous. It would dwarf Queensdale Palace. Arches line the walkway, opening into the central area, still obscured by mist. My mind starts to hop around, but I press back the questions that want to leap out of my mouth. I breathe. I keep walking.

Down another stairway, another walkway. Now each arch has a large, pale moonstone glowing from a triangular stone at its apex. The faint luminescence is coming from these. We descend more levels, each one narrower than the one before.

We arrive at the bottom of the valley, or castle. Encircled by a wide strip of mossy grass is the pool of the god TAN. It looks like an ordinary pond, still obscured by the last tendrils of mist.

Gundega takes the cord from around my waist and sets it aside, together with the one connecting me with Maelys. The thirteen Guardians form a wide circle around the edge of the grotto.

I take my place beside Maelys, who stands and gazes into the pool. Today she doesn't wear her Youthfulness glamour, and she looks tiny, skeletal, almost vulnerable, without her headdress and jewellery. Her silver hair hangs loose over her plain gown of pale, lustrous green. Her feet are covered with soft slippers, which she kicks off. She bows her head, for once looking almost humble, but she's groping in the folds of her skirt. She takes a small bag from a pocket and removes an ordinary looking cup the size and shape of a tulip.

She presents it to me with both hands and declaims the buzzing, ceremonial words. "Receive this Queen's gift from the last of the gods, made from air, earth, fire, wood, water, and starlight. The god TAN awakens from her three-hundred-year sleep to fill it with her essence, and the essence of the Queens who have come before us." Her voice is sonorous, but as she watches me take the vessel, her dark, almost black eyes hold a strange glitter.

CHAPTER 49

We wait. Between the fasting and the early start, I'm feeling light-headed. But I remember to breathe, and stand tall as I would when getting ready to dance.

The vessel nested in my hands fascinates me. I *feel* its substance. Its outer surface is like roughly textured silk and wood woven together. The inside looks cloudy, like nothing. But then I *see*. It's like I'm floating in an iridescent cloud above the pool, above this valley, above the Land.

My eyes are filled with all colors and none, colors never seen by mortal beings, colors of the lost gods. My vision coalesces and for a moment, I *see* everything. Everything that ever was. I see the gods and giants making their insane wars. I see tremendous companies of dragons incinerating everything in their path. I see them perish in the inferno that once was Dragons' Peak. It's like in the tapestries, but real. I see a young Fae Queen tenderly cradling the last god, here in this same grotto, gently supporting her down into the pool. I see the Humans settling their river valley. I see a young Maelys, weeping in anguish. I see a boy watching an enormous egg shake and crack open. I see...

Gundega touches my hand, breaking up the vision. Maelys motions her to stand back, then continues to gaze into the water, which is now a clear pool, but so deep that I can't see the bottom.

I try to return to the vision, but I'm getting restless. I start thinking forward to the equinox of spring three hundred years from now, when it will be my turn to guide a new Fae Queen to her destiny. I shiver with the thought. I still don't understand how Maelys became so mean and bitter, but I resolve not to let that happen to me.

I wonder what Caden is doing. I hope he's with the court, who must be arriving up above by now to wait for me. Is it still misty up there? My body remembers his touch, and now I shiver with a flare of desire that makes my wing nubs tingle. I look up at the brightening sky above the deep cone we climbed down into.

A finger of sunlight touches the topmost of the moonstones that lighted our way, and the light suddenly spirals down from all the moonstones like tiny suns racing towards us. My wing nubs throb and release as the lights reach the pool.

Maelys' wings are also unfurled, draping loosely down the back of her gown. She takes a step closer to the water, but then turns away from me. It looks like she's tracing a spell on the front of her body, but I can't see it. Then she motions me to come and stand beside her, looking at me again with that peculiar gleam in her eyes.

There is a tiny ripple in the pool. She raises her arms and calls, "A Queen is here, Beloved of the ages. She gives herself to you that the Land may be healed. She gives herself to you that all beings may live peacefully." She enunciates each word carefully, the ritual summoning of TAN, the last god. I memorized it as part of my initiation. Her voice buzzes on in the ancient tongue and I stand suspended, staring into the deep water, cupping the vessel in both my hands. I wonder how TAN will appear.

Maelys takes a slow step toward the edge of the water, but suddenly she turns and snatches the vessel out of my hands, her face distorted in a grimace of loathing. Her grating voice snarls at me. “You can’t steal this from me, stupid girl. This vessel is mine. The elixir is mine. The dragons are mine. Their blood is mine.”

I’m stunned as her bony claw reaches to clasp my wrist.

But Gundega is right behind me. She roars like a cougar and grabs Maelys’ elbow. She tries to pull her around and seize the vessel. But the shockingly strong old Queen grips her arm and hurtles Gundega forward. Time stops as she goes flying, and the vessel goes flying. They seem to float in the air before both it and my companion plunge into the water and vanish into the depths of the pool.

I don’t even have time to be shocked when Maelys clutches for me again. “You’ll never be queen. You’re the one who’s going to the pool.”

My mind is frozen, but my body knows how to react. Without conscious thought, I fling her hands away from me and *flicker* behind her. Maelys spins around to me and screeches. Bony hands shaking, she traces a Compliance spell in the air, not knowing that her herbs to keep me docile have gone to waste.

She lunges toward me, reaching into her skirt. She pulls out the same small knife she wielded at the dragons. With her other hand, she flings balls of light at me to try and blind me. She shouts incoherent words, repeatedly stabbing the knife in the air towards me and grasping to pull me into the water.

I *flicker* again to get farther away from her. I'm not a fighter, but I have to do something. I *flicker* back to her side, where her hand clutches the knife. I grab her wrist to try and make her drop it. But she twists and grabs my other hand to pull me into the water. I brace myself against her weird strength, still holding the wrist that has the knife. I grip and shake it as hard as I can. She drops the knife. It flips over once and lands with its tip on her bare foot.

She lets go of me and screams, her shrill voice frenzied. "No! Poison! Get it off me!" She lunges into the pool, trying to wash it off. But whatever the poison is, it's potent, and the extraordinary strength she just had abandons her. She staggers deeper into the water, unable to stop herself, and starts to sink.

Maelys turns toward me one last time, her pinched face now contorted in terror, bony hands reaching out. My reflex is to help, but I hold back. I witness with dry eyes as she slowly submerges and then disappears, as she was meant to.

I stand and stare at the fading ripple until the surface of the water is smooth again. The Guardians are still circling the pool. A few of them have taken a couple of steps toward us. But it all happened so quickly they had no time to react. Maelys has returned to the god, and fulfilled her destiny.

And now I must face mine. Except I can't. *Gundega. The elixir!* The vessel is at the bottom of the pool. I look helplessly into the water for the elixir that would heal the land. It's not there.

There will be no healing of the land. There will be no pilgrimage to Dragon's End Mountain. There will be no communing with its hot essence, no curing of the poison, which will continue to seep out of the mountain. It will spread everywhere. There will be no joy, no beauty. Eventually the Land will sicken and die, and everyone with it, just as foreseen in the Venerable Dame's tapestry.

I slump down at the edge of the pool. I'm numb, bleak, empty. I don't feel the soft grass, nor the emerging warmth of the day. I can only feel the devastation careening toward me.

I look down and find the green stone in my hand. It's glowing again, but I can't think of any use for it, so I toss it listlessly into the water. The jade stone sinks into the pool, more slowly than a stone should, its soft radiance pulsing rhythmically. As it settles, its faint illumination reveals the vessel made of air, earth, fire, wood, water, and starlight, far below, resting on its side at the silty bottom.

CHAPTER 50

I sit there for a long time, lost in despair, oblivious to the crescent of Guardians bearing witness in silence around me. Finally, chest hollow, limbs heavy, I pick myself up and slowly turn to look for the spiral path leading back up the valley. Up to the Fae waiting at the top. My Fae. I'm their Queen. Their failed Queen. Doomed before I even started. How will I face them? How will I tell them? How can I possibly lead them?

I sigh and take a slow step. But as I turn, the corner of my eye catches a small flutter on the water. I look more closely and the ripple increases. Then a scrawny arm reaches out, the vessel in its hand. It's filled with something that bubbles and shimmers. My heart leaps. I know that arm. It's Gundega, she's come back. I lean forward to pull her out.

The vessel of air, earth, fire, wood, water, and starlight is resting in the palm of her hand. She gently pushes it into the air towards me. It glides into my reaching hands, and Gundega's arm withdraws back into the glassy depths. *NO, Gundega!* But she's gone. My gruff companion. The broken Fae. She came back to save the Land, and now she's gone.

But the vessel resting in my hands tugs at my attention. I gaze into the frothy elixir. My tears for Gundega fall into the cup, but the elixir continues to effervesce.

I know what I have to do. I raise it to my mouth. I take a sip, but as it touches my lips, of its own accord, the elixir slides down my throat in one large but smooth gulp. It has no taste except… *everything*.

All flavors burst forth inside my mouth and caress the surfaces of my tongue. They course throughout my body, and I *taste* all the feasts ever celebrated, all the cakes and fruits, the plain gruels, the meads and juices, the sweet, the tart, the bland, the bitter herbs that give savor or medicine. Even the taste of meat, which doesn't disgust me as I apprehend the varying needs of different beings.

Before I could see everything in the vessel, but now I *feel* everything. I am filled with warmth, and coolness. I *feel* the life of the land, of spring greening throughout the forest, of the burrows where young creatures ready to be born. Of water coursing down the mountain, or lapping on the shore.

I'm filled with all emotions. With bliss and sadness. With passion and anger and jealousy. With power and frailty. I *feel* with all the denizens of the land, the Fae, the Humans, the elves, the elementals, with all the creatures that run, or fly, or climb, or slither. With the great cacophony of all that is the Land, joined in a perfectly synchronized dance. I am. I am air, earth, fire, wood, water, and starlight. I am everything.

I'm lying on the ground that is now the same as my body. My spirit essence sinks into the earth, down to its core, and I rest there for a small eternity.

I *feel* Dragons' End mountain summoning me, urging me to hasten, to bring it a taste of my blood. I *feel* the land, thrusting its green tendrils up out of the earth. I *feel* the god, TAN, melting back into repose, enfolding Gundega, no longer broken, restored to her Fae nature, merging her essence with the god.

I *feel* Maelys, fading, shrinking, disappearing into a final tiny nugget of hatred. I *feel* the Fae, all the Clans, waiting for their new Queen to restore harmony. I *feel* the Humans, even the Raiders, wanting to prosper and be safe. I *feel*....

I'm walking slowly up the stairs, now illuminated by the warm radiance of midday. It's a long climb, and I breathe deeply, reflecting on all that waits for me at the top. The Land. The mountain. The Clans. The Humans. Caden. My parents. Kairon. The attendants. The Court. So many things, and so much that I'll have to learn.

As I climb, the air warms and brightens me, and bubbles of hope flutter in my chest. It's an enormous task. And I'm not Marielle. But I am enough. I have what I need. I have... everything.

At the top of the path, the air has cleared, revealing the magnificent castle this once was. I step up into the clearing and they are all there, waiting for me. They hail their new Queen. I bow to them, to acknowledge the life of service I'm taking on.

At the edge of the clearing, a young dragon waits, extending his wing.

The end

Beatrix

ACKNOWLEDGEMENTS

I owe an enormous debt of gratitude to the many people who helped me write this first novel. Apparently, it takes a village.

Aren X. Tulchinsky of the Vancouver Manuscript intensive, a published author and screenwriter, and a wise and kind writing teacher, coached me from first draft through to draft three at the beginning of the pandemic. He taught me how to feed my imagination, bringing a new richness to dialog, settings, and characters.

Eric Maizel, a widely published psychologist and creativity coach, finally convinced me of the value of writing every day. With the help and encouragement of his Get Your Book Written class and support group, I actually did it.

Jessica Loftus, final editor of my book when I thought it was finished, gently pointed out the flaws I knew were there but had been trying to avoid.

Priscilla Boucher and I went for many walks around Queen Elizabeth Park, where she offered insightful comments as I created and discarded scenes and characters. We especially enjoyed watching Sir Quack, the white drake, who occasionally added his thoughts, too.

Pat Rusnell tossed many ideas around with me. We were like seals playing with colored balls just to see how the drops of water would sparkle off them. We discussed many important matters, including the significance of dragon poop to the evolution of the Fae. Pat was my first beta reader. Her friendship and encouragement helped me through some tough times.

Beta readers Earle Peach, John Hawkins, Stephen Douglas, gave honest feedback, kindly pointed out discontinuities and plot holes, and convinced me to add a few more commas.

Just Write Meetup friends provided an atmosphere conducive to writing as we met in the coffee shop three times a week. Especially Terry Reid and Mark O'Meara, who were several steps ahead of me in the publishing process, and generously shared many resources for getting our respective books written and out there.

Performance party friends heard various chapters and cheered me on with enthusiasm while the work was in progress.

My dear friends who encouraged me, believed in me, and pre-purchased copies of the book before it was even half written: Andy Rose, Brad Leslie, Callum MacLeod, Candace Plattor, Heidi Rose, Mandy Pants, Mike O'Brien, Pat Rusnell, Priscilla Boucher, Shelagh Smith, Silvi Wool.

And finally, Robin Hobb, author of the astonishing and inspiring Elderling series of novels that opened up a whole new realm of possibility in fantasy writing.

Manufactured by Amazon.ca
Bolton, ON

38140403R00187